Allocating Pensions to Younger People

Gregory Ponthiere

Allocating Pensions to Younger People

Towards a Social Insurance against a Short Life

palgrave
macmillan

Gregory Ponthiere
UCLouvain
Louvain-la-Neuve, Belgium

ISBN 978-3-031-24747-7 ISBN 978-3-031-24748-4 (eBook)
https://doi.org/10.1007/978-3-031-24748-4

This Palgrave Macmillan imprint is published by the registered company Springer Nature Switzerland AG
The registered company address is: Gewerbestrasse 11, 6330 Cham, Switzerland

What foolish obliviousness to our mortality
to put off wise plans to our fiftieth and sixtieth year,
and to want to begin life from a point that few have reached!

Seneca, On the Shortness of Life, III.

Preface

This book is an English version of *Retraites et justice sociale. La logique de la retraite inversée* published by L'autreface in 2022, an essay which synthesizes a decade of research on the construction of a fair welfare state in the context of risky and unequal longevity. In that particular context, all persons know that they will die in the future, but no one—neither individuals, nor the state—knows exactly *when* one will die. Some unlucky individuals will turn out to die prematurely, whereas others, luckier, will enjoy a long life. How can one construct just institutions—in particular a just welfare state—under such circumstances?

In the quest for social justice under risky and unequal longevity, a decisive moment was the publication of the article 'Compensating the dead' in the *Journal of Mathematical Economics* (2014), an article co-authored with Marc Fleurbaey and Marie-Louise Leroux. This article demonstrates that the compensation of victims of a short life is possible, despite the impossibility to identify short-lived persons when they are still alive, and despite the impossibility to compensate short-lived individuals when they are dead. The article 'Compensating the dead' shows that these two obstacles can be overcome by improving the situation of *all* young persons, because the set of young persons includes the (unidentified) subset of the few persons who will die prematurely in the future. Age-based discrimination favouring the young can, by transferring resources from good states of nature (long life) to bad states of nature (short life), provide compensation to the short-lived, thus laying the foundations of a social insurance against the risk of a premature death. The universal uncertainty about the length of life and the ideal of social justice are not irreconcilable.

After the publication of 'Compensating the dead', the subsequent years of research were dedicated to applying the same insurance rationale to richer economic environments, including the labour market. This research gave rise to the publication of other articles, such as 'Fair retirement under risky lifetime' (with Marc Fleurbaey, Marie-Louise Leroux and Pierre Pestieau, published in *International Economic Review*, 2016), which focuses on the selection of the optimal age of exit from work, 'Working time regulations, unequal lifetimes and fairness' (with Marie-Louise Leroux, published in *Social Choice and Welfare*, 2018), which examines the design of working time regulations under a fixed duration of the career, and 'A theory of reverse retirement' (published in *Journal of Public Economic Theory*, 2020), which studies the introduction of an initial retirement period before work. The latter article inaugurated research on reverse retirement systems, i.e., pension systems where young adults enjoy, during a period preceding their career, pension allowances financed by the work of older workers (a kind of reversal of existing pension systems). Such pension systems are 'reverse' in the precise sense that these systems involve not only monetary transfers from the young to the old (as usual), but, also, transfers from senior persons to junior persons.

Whereas these articles were published in mathematical economics journals, the present essay aims at presenting, in a more informal manner—accessible to a large audience—the key intuitions justifying the construction of a social insurance against the risk of a premature death, as well as the specific role that a system of reverse retirement can play in the realization of social justice in the context of risky and unequal longevity. In this essay, I argue that, in light of the large harm due to a premature death, it is socially desirable to construct a new pillar of the welfare state, dedicated to a social insurance against the risk of a short life. It is shown that, under the demographic and technological conditions of advanced economies, a reverse retirement system constitutes a necessary component of a social insurance against a short life. The construction of a reverse retirement system is needed to reconcile, on the one hand, the universal uncertainty about the duration of life and, on the other hand, the requirements of social justice.

In order to provide a defence of reverse retirement as a social insurance against a short life, this essay has to cross disciplinary boundaries between economics and philosophy, and to construct a kind of analytical bridge connecting—currently separated—branches of knowledge, such as the philosophical literature on the badness of death and the economics literature on the welfare state and pension reforms. Walking along an interdisciplinary bridge is not as comfortable as remaining within one specific disciplinary field, but this difficult task is the price to pay to be able to defend a non-marginal reorientation of the welfare state. Partially reversing pension systems is not about changing one parameter of pension systems. This reform involves a major departure from existing social protection and, as such, requires more substantial justification. This is the task that this essay tries to carry out.

My first acknowledgements go to my coauthors Marc Fleurbaey, Marie-Louise Leroux and Pierre Pestieau, who accompanied me in long parts of this intellectual journey to the construction of a social insurance against a short life.

This work benefited also, through the publication of the above-mentioned articles (and other articles and book chapters), of the comments and suggestions of other researchers, to whom I would like to express my gratitude (in alphabetical order): Geir Asheim, Borja Barragué, Arno Baurin, Nicolas Brando, Arnold Chassagnon, Helmuth Cremer, Manuel De Araujo E Sa Valente, Philippe De Donder, Pierre Devolder, Joseph Ferret-Mas, Nathalie Frogneux, Alexia Furnkranz-Prskawetz, Axel Gosseries, Nicolas Gravel, Kevin Hartmann Cortes, Jean Hindriks, Marcus Knell, Jean-François Laslier, François Maniquet, André Masson, Fabien Moizeau, Patrick Moyes, Hervé Pourtois, Patrick Savidan, Erik Schokkaert, Vincent Touzé, Philippe Van Parijs, Vincent Vandenberghe, Bertrand Wigniolle, Stéphane Zuber and Danièle Zwarthoed. I would like also to thank Sandrine Levasseur from the editions *L'autreface* for her investment in this project. Finally, I would like also to express my gratitude to the editor Ellie Duncan from Palgrave Macmillan.

Brussels, Belgium
October 2022

Gregory Ponthiere

Contents

List of Tables

CHAPTER 1

Introduction: *homo economicus, homo moriturus*

Abstract This short essay defends a reorientation of the welfare state, which takes the form of the construction of a new 'pillar' of social protection: a social insurance against the risk of premature death, that is, the risk of a short life. Nowadays, such a social insurance does not exist within modern welfare states. Possible causes for this non-existence include a double *invisibility*: on the one hand, the invisibility of the victims of premature death, whose interests are quickly forgotten once they have disappeared from the social field; on the other hand, the invisibility of the loss due to premature death, which is hard to observe or measure (when a person dies, this implies also the disappearance of her life projects and her life goals, all the things she would have done provided she did not die so early).

Keywords Welfare State · Social insurance · Premature death · Insurance against short life · Invisibility

In the twenty-first century, the idea of a basic income dedicated to the youth has become a key ingredient of debates about the reform of the welfare state. The philosophical foundations of such a basic income for the young are—unlike the foundations for the *universal* basic income—still underdeveloped, despite the fact that these foundations matter for the

G. Ponthiere, *Allocating Pensions to Younger People*,
https://doi.org/10.1007/978-3-031-24748-4_1

desirability and for the political acceptability of this reform. The present essay shows that it is possible to provide ethical foundations for a basic income dedicated to the youth, neither as a kind of social insertion device, nor as a project-stipend, but, rather, as the keystone of a social insurance against the risk of a short life. The construction of an insurance against a short life requires to rethink the welfare state and, in particular, the design of pension systems.

Existing pension systems (and their rivals) share a common property: they reserve retirement for individuals who reach old ages (usually 60 years or more). Retirement—a period of leisure time and consumption without work—is the privilege of persons who have the chance to have a long life.[1] A premature death deprives automatically individuals from the pleasures of being retired.[2] Our world is fundamentally unjust: while individuals who enjoy a long life benefit also from pension allowances during several decades, unlucky persons who die prematurely cannot even reach the retirement age. Worse: the persons who die prematurely have often spent many years at work, paying mandatory contributions that benefit to the lucky ones who enjoy a long period of retirement. Existing pension systems share an unattractive feature: by (implicitly) redistributing resources from short-lived persons to long-lived persons, these systems tend to amplify or exacerbate social injustice due to unequal longevity.[3]

The injustice caused by longevity inequalities has been quasi-absent in the debates about the reform of the French pension system in 2019, which was about the transition from multiple sectorial pension systems

[1] Throughout this essay, I will, following a long tradition in economics, use the term 'leisure time' in a broad way, as a substitute for 'free time'. 'Leisure time' so defined includes all time that is not dedicated to working.

[2] By a 'premature death', I mean a death that takes place before the age of 60 years, and which is of involuntary nature (the death may be due to an accident, or to a chronic or acute disease). In France, about 10% of men and 4% of women die before having reached the age of 60 years.

[3] That injustice concerns all retirement systems. In fully funded pension systems (where pension rights are a function of the accumulated saving during the career), that transfer takes place between individuals who belong to the same cohort (but having unequal lifetimes). In pay-as-you-go pension systems (where the pension allowances of a given year are funded by contributions paid during the same year by workers), that transfer is done from young persons (who will turn out to be short-lived) towards older persons (and thus living longer) who belong to earlier cohorts.

to a unique pension system based on notional accounts.[4] This absence is probably due to the invisibility of the victims of that injustice. Once dead, the persons are no longer part of the population interviewed by journalists, targeted by political speeches or studied by social scientists.[5] But the invisibility of the victims of a premature death does not justify that the society ignores the injustice faced by the short-lived.[6]

This essay proposes a reorientation of the welfare state aimed at reducing these injustices. This reorientation would consist in constructing a social insurance against a short life. This new social insurance would take the form of an inversion or reversal of pension systems: under a reverse pension system, a pension allowance would be paid to young adults *before* they start their career, by postponing both the age of entrance in the labour market and the age of exit from the labour market. Under such a reverse retirement system, retirement would no longer be the privilege of persons who have a long life, but would become a reality for everyone.[7] By generalizing access to retirement to all individuals, reverse retirement systems would make our societies less unfair.

Reverse retirement? Is this serious? A few years ago, the satiric TV show 'Présipauté de Grosland' on Canal+, which consists of TV news programme presenting the latest miscellaneous facts of the fictitious state of Grosland, showed a utopian reform of reverse retirement. In that TV show, one could see unhealthy elderly persons bringing—with their tired

[4] A notional pension system takes into account the productive efforts of workers by means of a fictitious account, that virtual capital being converted into an annuity at the end of the career (Lavigne 2013). Concerning the transition to a notional pension system, see Bozio and Piketty (2008) and criticisms by Sterdyniak (2009).

[5] This invisibility is illustrated by the absence, in English, of a word that designs the 'persons who have a short life', whereas there exist many words—such as 'centenarian'—to refer to 'persons who have a long life'.

[6] On the invisibility of victims of premature death, a classical reference is Sen (1998).

[7] Throughout this essay, we will use the term 'reverse retirement' to refer to pension systems where the pension allowances paid to young adults are funded by the work of the old, and, as such, involve a reversal of the logic of standard pension systems. Whereas classical retirement refers to the fact that senior persons retire or withdraw from the labour market, reverse retirement involves also some withdrawal from work, but to the advantage of young adults. Reverse retirement should be distinguished from other reforms of the welfare state, such as the basic income, the universal capital endowment or sabbatical leaves. These alternative settings do not necessarily imply that young adults stay away from the labour market, unlike reverse retirement.

body—some food dishes to smiling young individuals sitting in a restaurant. Is such a situation just? How could reverse retirement contribute to social justice?

The logic of reverse retirement is so distant from our world that it makes us laugh. But these laughs should be taken seriously: these reveal the presence of stereotypical representations, which prevent us from understanding what ageing consists of in the twenty-first century, and, hence, hide some possible futures for our ageing societies. These representations are obstacles that disturb our understanding of all challenges raised by retirement systems.

A first obstacle concerns the work of the *senior*. Stereotypes about the elderly are long-lasting: old persons are generally supposed to be tired by the passage of time, weak, clumsy, overwhelmed by events or by new technologies. These stereotypes make us laugh when considering the idea of maintaining old individuals at work. But reality is different: the biological age—the level of physical and cognitive abilities—is largely disconnected from the chronological age—the age deduced from the date of birth.[8] Being 60-year-old in 2020 is not equivalent, from the perspective of abilities and skills, to being 60-year-old in 1950. It would be a mistake to reject reverse retirement because of age stereotypes.

Other obstacles stand in front of us. The statement 'short-lived persons suffer from an injustice' is not trivial. That statement is in conflict with a double invisibility: on the one hand, the invisibility of the victims of a premature death and, on the other hand, the invisibility of the harm and losses caused by a premature death. The invisibility of the persons who have a short life influences the way in which we think about social protection and pension systems. Our attention is laid on the living persons, on the individuals who are still around, whereas the interests of the persons who died prematurely are quickly forgotten. But the invisibility concerns also the harm underwent by the victims of a premature death.[9] A premature death, by depriving the person of achievements and life accomplishments, causes a serious harm. The evil of an early death depends on the quantity and the quality of years that would have been lived provided the premature death did not take place. Although the evil of an early death

[8] Concerning the relations between biological ages and chronological ages, see Ponthiere (2017).

[9] See Sen (1998) on the invisible deprivation caused by premature death.

is substantial, the associated harm is invisible: when a person dies, all her dreams, her life projects and her aspirations also disappear. The invisibility of the harm caused by a premature death also disturbs our understanding of injustices due to unequal longevity.

Thinking about more just pension systems requires overcoming stereotypes and primary images—the invisibility of victims and the invisibility of harms due to a premature death—what Gaston Bachelard called epistemological obstacles.[10] The construction of a fair pension system requires taking seriously a fundamental feature of human beings: before being a *homo economicus*—a rational agent satisfying his preferences with the lowest efforts—human beings are what Vladimir Jankélévitch called a *homo moriturus*—a being whose destiny is to die.[11] Lifetime is the scarcest of all resources and, also, a resource available in an unknown quantity: one may have far less remaining lifetime than one believes. The design of a fair retirement system requires taking into account the temporal finiteness of men and women, who should be described as *homo moriturus* rather than as *homo economicus*.

Constructing a fair pension system is a complex problem of social architecture, which raises numerous difficulties. First of all, the design of a just pension system requires clarifying what we mean by 'social justice', that is, adopting some principles concerning just institutions. The difference principle formulated by John Rawls in his *Theory of Justice* states that institutions should give priority, when allocating material resources, to the most disadvantaged persons.[12] But in the context of universal uncertainty about the length of life, it is far from straightforward to be able to identify the most disadvantaged persons.

In a society peopled of *homo moriturus*, the identification of the most disadvantaged persons raises serious challenges.[13] No one knows how long one will live. Statistical institutes compute average lengths of life within groups (for instance, life expectancies by socio-economic group or education level), but they cannot forecast the length of life for each distinct person. The construction of a just retirement system in a society peopled of *homo moriturus* is thus made difficult by the impossibility of

[10] See Bachelard (1938).

[11] See Jankelevitch (1977).

[12] See Rawls (1971).

[13] On these difficulties, see Fleurbaey et al. (2014).

identifying the persons who will die prematurely and who will turn out to be the most disadvantaged by the lottery of life.[14] Unfortunately, when these disadvantaged persons are identified—at the time of their death—it is often too late to try to improve their situation: these persons are then dead, and it is almost impossible to do things that can correct the injustice they suffer from.

The universal uncertainty about the length of life and the requirement of social justice seem to be, at first glance, incompatible. The problem of social architecture appears to be without solution: if the victims of the injustice—the short-lived—cannot be identified when they are alive, but only once they are dead (when it is too late to improve their situation), it seems impossible to correct the injustice caused by a premature death. Our societies would thus have no other choice than to give up the ideal of justice: one could simply not fight against injustices caused by longevity inequalities.

Existing pension systems have given up the ideal of social justice. In our societies, the persons who die prematurely are penalized twice: once by the mere fact of having a short life and another time by existing pension systems. Actually, the shortness of life prevents individuals from pursuing their life goals, whose realization requires some time. But individuals who die prematurely are also the victims of a second injustice: during their short life, they often contributed to pension systems that benefit to the long-lived, who will enjoy a long retirement period. Regressive monetary transfers from the most disadvantaged—the short-lived—to persons enjoying a better situation (the long-lived): this is the exact opposite of what social justice requires. Hence, the short-lived suffer from a double injustice: to the first injustice—the shortness of their life—is added a second injustice: monetary transfers towards the lucky long-lived. Our world is really badly made!

However, this unattractive picture is not the only possible one. This essay aims at demonstrating that, if one revisits the construction of a fair retirement system, there is no dead end. It is possible to reconcile the universal uncertainty about the length of life and the requirement of social justice. The solution takes the form of a reverse retirement system.

[14] There exist various measures of the risk about the duration of life. For instance, Meyer and Ponthiere (2020) quantify this risk by means of Shannon's lifetime entropy index to the basis 2. This index is the mathematical expectation of the quantity of information (in bits) revealed by the event of a death at a particular age.

By reversing pension systems, and by allowing everyone to enjoy a retirement period at the beginning of the adult life—and not only at the end of life, for the luckiest persons—one can neutralize the second source of injustice. The retirement period would no longer be the privilege of the long-lived, but could be enjoyed by everyone. Even better, the reverse retirement system would also reduce the size of the first injustice, by improving the (short) life enjoyed by the persons who will turn out to die prematurely. There exists no logical incompatibility between our nature of *homo moriturus* and social justice.

The present essay aims at describing and defending this path allowing for the reconciliation of the universal uncertainty about the length of life and the requirement of social justice. A new welfare state is possible: it will include—in addition to health insurance, unemployment insurance, etc.—a new pillar: a social insurance against the risk of a short life, which takes the form of a reverse retirement system. This insurance device will reduce the injustices caused by unequal longevities by offering compensation to the victims of a short life.

Our defence of reverse retirement will take place in three steps.

Chapter 2 will study the existence—and the measurement—of the welfare loss caused by a premature death. The persons who die prematurely are invisible victims, but this invisibility should not be an obstacle preventing the quantification of the injustice they suffer. Chapter 2 will propose an analysis of the nature and the size of the harm due to a short life, as well as of the determinants of that harm.

The social desirability and the feasibility of an insurance against the risk of a short life will be examined in Chapter 3. I will defend the idea that a just society should provide a compensation to the short-lived persons, and that this compensation can take place despite the non-identification of the persons who will die prematurely, and despite the (quasi) impossibility of compensating these persons once these are dead. These two obstacles can be overcome by subordinating social institutions to a simple maxim of resource allocation along the ages of life: concentrating the 'good things of life' at young ages and the 'less good things of life' at older ages.

Finally, Chapter 4 will defend that the construction of a social insurance against a short life requires designing a reverse retirement system. Chapter 4 will examine issues relative to the financial viability of such an insurance device, as well as the selection of ages of entry and exit of the labour market. This chapter will also study the design of a transition path from existing pension systems to reverse pension systems. The analysis of demographic and technological conditions suggests that our societies benefit nowadays from circumstances that are more favourable than ever before in order to introduce a reverse retirement system.

In sum, this essay defends that it is possible to construct new institutions in order to bring more justice in our societies, despite risky and unequal longevities. In its current form, the welfare state organizes a social insurance against the risk of disease, against the risk of unemployment, and against the risk of old-age poverty. But the welfare state does not insure citizens against the most dramatic of all risks: the risk of a short life. Reverse retirement would allow for a reduction of social injustices caused by premature deaths. By allowing all young adults—including the ones who will die prematurely in the future—to enjoy an initial period of retirement before starting their career, reverse retirement would make the unlucky short-lived better off and would thus be one major step towards more social justice. This essay is a defence of reverse retirement and, more generally, a defence of a more humane economy, where the acknowledgement of the finiteness of Man—*homo moriturus* rather than *homo economicus*—and the requirement of social justice would govern the organization of our institutions and would structure our lives.

References

Bachelard, Gaston. 1938. *La formation de l'esprit scientifique*. Paris: Vrin.

Bozio, Antoine, and Thomas Piketty. 2008. *Pour un nouveau système de retraites*. Paris: Editions rue d'Ulm.

Fleurbaey, Marc, Marie-Louise Leroux, and Gregory Ponthiere. 2014. 'Compensating the Dead'. *Journal of Mathematical Economics* 51: 28–41.

Jankelevitch, Vladimir. 1977. *La mort*. Paris: Flammarion.

Lavigne, Anne. 2013. *Economie des retraites*. Paris: Editions La Découverte.

Meyer, Patrick, and Gregory Ponthiere. 2020. 'Human Lifetime Entropy in a Historical Perspective (1750–2014)'. *Cliometrica* 14: 129–167.

Ponthiere, Gregory. 2017. *Economie du vieillissement*. Paris: Editions La Découverte.

Rawls, John. 1971. *A Theory of Justice*. Cambridge: Harvard University Press.

Sen, Amartya. 1998. 'Mortality as an Indicator of Economic Success and Failure'. *Economic Journal* 100: 1–21.

Sterdyniak, Henri. 2009. 'Retraites: à la recherche de solutions miracles'. *Revue De l'OFCE* 109: 109–140.

CHAPTER 2

The Evil of a Premature Death

Abstract The existence of harm due to a short life is a necessary condition for the construction of a social insurance against premature death: in the absence of such harm, there would be no justification for insuring all citizens against a short life. But the specific nature of the event 'death of a person'—it implies that the person disappears—tends to make the characterization of the associated damage complex. This chapter examines the issue of the existence of harm due to premature death, by revisiting some arguments supporting the neutrality of death from the perspective of the person who dies. For that purpose, this chapter presents and critically assesses several arguments by Epicurus, Lucretius and Seneca, as well as criticisms of these arguments by modern analytical philosophers such as Nagel, Parfit and Broome. Based on these investigations, it is concluded that death is generally not neutral for the person who dies: death harms the person, to an extent that depends on the quantity and the quality of life-years that would have been lived in the absence of the event of premature death. The existence of such harm tends to open the questions of the social desirability and the feasibility of constructing a social insurance against premature death, questions examined in Chapter 3.

Keywords Death · Premature death · Harm · Evil of death · Deprivation account

G. Ponthiere, *Allocating Pensions to Younger People*,
https://doi.org/10.1007/978-3-031-24748-4_2

Il Sogno di Una Cosa tells the story of the lives of Nini Infant, Eligio Pereisson and Milio Bortolus in Post-War Italy (1948–1949). In the doldrums of Frioul, these three young friends try to live their lives, inhabited by an imprecise dream. This novel by Pier Paolo Pasolini ends up tragically, with the premature death of Eligio Pereisson. His body being weakened by long hours worked in a quarry, Eligio dies surrounded by his family and friends, who can no longer recognize him. 'It was no longer Eligio, that boy lying in the little bed in the hospital common room. The ravaged face, the long hair, the shoulders that protruded from the sheet seemed to be that of a 13-year old'.[1] His father was aware of Eligio's deteriorating health and asked Eligio to stop going to the mine. Eligio replied: 'And the shoes for Onorino, and the apron for the mother, what will we buy them with?'[2] The life of Eligio Pereisson was short, too short to allow him to realize the—still imprecise—dream that inhabited him.

The premature death of the young Eligio Pereisson has caused a great evil for his family and for his friends. But can we say that this premature death has also caused harm to Eligio Pereisson himself? More generally, does a short-lived person suffer from a harm or a loss? If yes, what are the determinants of what is being lost in the case of a premature death?

In order to avoid any confusion, let us stress that we raise here the question of the existence of harm for the person who dies prematurely, and leave aside the distinct problem of the existence of harm for the relatives of the deceased. This second question admits a straightforward answer—the existence, in general, of harm for the relatives—and does not need to be explored here. This chapter will focus on the study of the existence of harm for the deceased and on the determinants of that harm.[3]

At first glance, it is tempting to provide a quick answer to that question, and to state that a short life does not cause any harm to the deceased person. Actually, a person who is dead does not feel anything and cannot suffer from not being there. For the same reason, a deceased person cannot be conscious of all losses caused by her death. Once deceased, Eligio Pereisson has no consciousness of anything and thus cannot feel

[1] See Pasolini (1965, p. 204) (translation by the author).

[2] See Pasolini (1965, p. 208) (translation by the author).

[3] Note that we study here the existence of harms caused by an involuntary premature death and leave aside the complex issue of suicide.

any suffering, any regrets, and cannot be affected by his death. Without any consciousness, the deceased person cannot be disappointed of having lost something.

Denying the existence of harm caused by a premature death seems to rely on common sense. Like Saint Thomas, the layman only wants to believe what he can see with his own eyes. The harm caused by a short life, if it exists, cannot be felt by the deceased. Nor can it be observed by the relatives surviving that person. Can one then believe in the existence of an invisible harm? If no one can see the harm, it must be that this harm does not exist.

However, primary impressions, as stressed by Bachelard, can often be misleading.[4] Yes, the deceased persons are not there and the harm they suffered from is invisible too. This is obvious. But one cannot deduce from this that the event of their death did not cause any harm to them. Such a deduction would make the visibility of harm a necessary condition for the existence of that harm, a questionable postulate.

In everyday life, when some events make us worse off, the harms caused by these events are often visible. A bump on the knee is a visible trace of the harm caused, for instance, by a fall on a bicycle. But can we deduce that the visibility of the harm is a necessary condition for the existence of the harm *in all cases*, whatever harms are? Can one generalize what we know for everyday life harms to the harm due to a premature death? One can have doubts about this. At the scale of a human life, a death is a singular event, and transposing what we know for other events of life to that particular life event is risky. Instead of trying questionable generalization, let us take some distance with respect to everyday life events and ordinary harms.

This chapter aims at operating such a distancing from our primary life experiences, in order to think about the existence of a harm caused by a short life. Starting from the occurrence of a premature death, we will ask the question of the existence, for the deceased person, of a harm caused by her death. Doing so, the coming pages will inevitably consider representations of death that humans have, across centuries, constructed. These mental schemes represent that singular event and have some corollaries for the existence—or the non-existence—of a harm caused by a short life.

[4] See Bachelard (1938).

The question of the existence of a harm caused by a premature death is almost as old as philosophy. In the fourth century BC, Epicurus argued, in his *Letter to Menoeceus*, that 'death is nothing for us'. Taking Epicurus's position as a starting point, we will analyse different theses concerning the existence—and the determinants—of the harm due to a short life. Beyond Epicurus, we will examine the positions defended by Lucretius and Seneca, who also defended—but for other reasons—the thesis of the neutrality of death. Then, after a short *détour* via the representations of human lifetime developed in the twentieth century by Wittgenstein and Bachelard, who describe the conditions for a possible neutrality of death, we will use contemporary analytical philosophy—in particular the works of Nagel, Parfit and Broome—to question the idea of a neutral death.

2.1 Epicurus: Death Does Not Matter for Us

The right attitude to adopt when facing death is only one facet—among others—of Epicurus's philosophy. The ultimate goal of that system of thought is to bring Man to a state of absence of suffering, a state known as *ataraxia*. The Epicurean wise man suffers from no pain (neither physical, nor mental). The quest for *ataraxia* requires to free individuals from their fears—including, among other things, the fear of death. For that purpose, Epicurus needs to demonstrate that the fear of death is not rational, that it should not be.[5]

The overall goal of reaching the state of *ataraxia* helps us understanding the view according to which 'death is nothing for us'. By defending that position, Epicurus aims at freeing individuals from the fear of death, in order to allow them to live a good life. For the sake of defending the neutrality of death, Epicurus uses two distinct arguments. The first one deals with the nature of the good and the bad, and their necessary relation with sensations. The second argument concerns the temporal location of the event of the death of a person.

The first argument is included in this well-known passage of the *Letter to Menoeceus*[6]:

[5] See Warren (2004).

[6] See Epicurus, *Letter to Menoeceus*, § 3.

> Become accustomed to the belief that death is nothing to us. For all good and evil consists in sensation, but death is deprivation of sensation [...]

Epicurus states that one should not be afraid of death, because death is not a cause of harm for the person who dies. Any good or bad involves a sensation. However, since death is the absence of all sensations, that event cannot be good or bad for the deceased.[7] That argument relies on three premises. First, a hedonistic conception of the good and the bad: the good and the bad are necessarily related to sensations (hedonism). Second, the postulate according to which the only manner for an event to cause harm to a person is to cause feelings of pain to that person.[8] Third, the postulate stating that death is the absence of any feeling or sensation.

The third premise being unquestionable, let us focus on the first two. Hedonism can be questioned, since this reduces human well-being to only *one* of its dimensions (feelings of pleasure or suffering). Welfare economics has well understood the cost of such a limitation of hedonism and considers utility as a measure of all what matters for a person, without reducing well-being to sensations only.[9] But hedonism is not sufficient to prove the neutrality of death. Another postulate is necessary: this states that the unique way for an event to deteriorate the situation of a person is to generate sensations of suffering for this person. That postulate excludes the possibility that an event harms a person by preventing the occurrence of feelings of pleasure.[10]

Let us now consider the second argument, also formulated in the *Letter to Menoeceus*[11]:

[7] Obviously, the death of a person can make other persons suffer. His death is something bad for these relatives. But not for the person who dies, because he cannot have any suffering once dead.

[8] That postulate is discussed by Broome (2004). We will discuss this premise later on in this chapter.

[9] See Pigou (1920) on early welfare economics. The evolution of the concept of 'utility' towards a numerical representation of preferences accounting for 'all what matters' for a person is discussed in Sen (1977).

[10] We will come back of that key point later on in this essay, when studying the works of John Broome.

[11] See Epicurus, *Letter to Menoeceus*, § 3.

> So death, the most terrifying of ills, is nothing to us, since so long as we exist, death is not with us; but when death comes, then we do not exist. It does not then concern either the living or the dead, since for the former it is not, and the latter are no more.

According to Epicurus, the death of a person does not concern her, because this event takes place outside her life. The events 'life' and 'death' of a person do not overlap along the time line, so that the event of the death of a person does not belong to her life. Thus that event cannot affect that person, nor penalize her. This implies that death is neutral for her.

That second argument is based on several premises. The first premise concerns the temporal location of the event of the death of a person and specifies that this event lies *outside* the life of that person. The second premise states that an event can only harm a person provided this event is temporally located *within* the life of that person.

The first premise looks plausible, but the second one is more demanding. It is not straightforward that all harms affecting a person must be associated with events that occur within her life. In particular, death may be the singular event that causes harm to a person while being localized outside the life of that person.[12] We will consider that issue in more details when studying the works of Thomas Nagel later on in this chapter.

To conclude, let us highlight an important corollary of the neutrality of death: a life can be good without being long. Since the death is neutral for the person who dies, a long life—a late death—is neither a necessary, nor a sufficient condition for having a good life. Epicurus wrote[13]:

> But the wise man neither seeks to escape life nor fears the cessation of life, for neither does life offend him nor does the absence of life seem to be any evil. And just as with food he does not seek simply the larger share and nothing else, but rather the most pleasant, so he seeks to enjoy not the longest period of time, but the most pleasant.

[12] A counterexample is given by the interest of altruistic persons for the well-being of future generations, well-being whose level depends on future events that are located outside the life of that person.

[13] See Epicurus, *Letter to Menoeceus*, § 4.

Epicurus considers that the quality of life is more important, from the perspective of a good life, than the quantity of life. This manner of representing the good life is at odds with modern economic theory, for which a short life is—under general conditions—regarded, *ceteris paribus*, as worse than a long life, on the grounds that the latter allows for the satisfaction of more desires than the former. In the economic theory of the lifecycle, the well-being associated with a life is defined as the (weighted) sum of all temporal utilities, along the period lived by the person. From that perspective, a longer life allows generally to accumulate more well-being, which leads to a life regarded as better.[14]

2.2 Lucretius: Symmetry, Satiation and Usufruct

In his poem *The Nature of Things*, Lucretius presents three arguments aimed at freeing humans from the 'scarecrow of death', this 'terror for no reason'.[15] The first argument—the one of symmetry—compares the situation of the deceased person after her death with the situation of that person before her birth[16]:

> Therefore death to us
> Is nothing, nor concerns us in the least,
> Since nature of mind is mortal evermore.
> And just as in the ages gone before
> We felt no touch of ill, when all sides round
> To battle came the Carthaginian host,
> And the times, shaken by tumultuous war,
> Under the aery coasts of arching heaven
> Shuddered and trembled, and all humankind
> Doubted to which the empery should fall
> By land and sea, thus when we are no more,
> When comes that sundering of our body and soul
> Through which we're fashioned to a single state,
> Verily naught to us, us then no more,
> Can come to pass, naught move our senses then—
> No, not if earth confounded were with sea,

[14] See Ponthiere (2017, Chapter 3).

[15] See Lucretius, *On the Nature of Things*, I, 50–55.

[16] See Lucretius, *On the Nature of Things*, III, 830–845.

> And sea with heaven.

That argument is based on two premises. First, events that preceded the life of a person do not make her suffer. Second, what holds for events taking place during the times of prenatal non-existence is also true for events taking place during the times of post-mortem non-existence (the symmetry postulate). The attractiveness of Lucretius's argument depends on the plausibility of the postulated premises. The first premise is actually implied by Epicurus's assumption according to which an event can cause harm to a person only if this is temporally located within the life of that person. We have already expressed above some questionings about that postulate. Regarding the symmetry postulate, it is, too, questionable, and we will discuss this in more detail when examining Derek Parfit's works.

The second argument proposed by Lucretius—the satiation argument—is formulated as follows[17]:

> Once more, if Nature
> Should of a sudden send a voice abroad,
> And her own self inveigh against us so:
> "Mortal, what hast thou of such grave concern
> That thou indulgest in too sickly plaints?
> Why this bemoaning and beweeping death?
> For if thy life aforetime and behind
> To thee was grateful, and not all thy good
> Was heaped as in sieve to flow away
> And perish unavailingly, why not,
> Even like a banqueter, depart the halls,
> Laden with life? why not with mind content
> Take now, thou fool, thy unafflicted rest?
> But if whatever thou enjoyed hath been
> Lavished and lost, and life is now offence,
> Why seekest more to add—which in its turn
> Will perish foully and fall out in vain?
> O why not rather make an end of life,
> Of labour?

To these persons who complain about being simple mortal beings, Lucretius proposes the following argument. Two alternatives can arise.

[17] See Lucretius, *On the Nature of Things*, III, 930–945.

Either the person succeeded in accomplishing lots of things in her life, so that adding a few more life-years will not change anything, since her life is already a success, or the person did not succeed in what she tried to achieve, so that adding a few more life-years will not bring anything better, because that extra lifetime will not allow her to achieve anything new. In these two cases, whatever the accomplished life was rich or poor, death is neutral, because it does not change anything to the goodness of life.

That argument supporting the neutrality of death relies on two premises. First, any life falls in one of the two categories proposed by Lucretius: either a life full of achievements, or a life without any achievement. This hypothesis is questionable: there exist a large number of lives that are neither so successful as to 'leave the table' while being satiated of life, nor such failures that one can leave the 'dinner of life' without regret. The second premise concerns the prevalence of a kind of satiation of life, whatever the life was a success or a failure. Assuming such a satiation of life—even if it is restricted to the two categories of lives considered by Lucretius—is questionable. Can one reach a satiation of life? Under which conditions? Or is the desire of living—a bit more—always active, whatever the circumstances are? These questionings tend to raise some scepticism towards the second argument of Lucretius.

Let us now consider the third argument proposed by Lucretius[18]:

> But now yield all that's alien to thine age,—
> Up, with good grace! make room for sons: thou must."
> Justly, I fancy, would she reason thus,
> Justly inveigh and gird: since ever the old
> Outcrowded by the new gives way, and ever
> The one thing from the others is repaired.
> Nor no man is consigned to the abyss
> Of Tartarus, the black. For stuff must be,
> That thus the after-generations grow,—
> Though these, their life completed, follow thee;
> And thus like thee are generations all—
> Already fallen, or some time to fall.
> So one thing from another rises ever;
> And in fee-simple life is given to none,
> But unto all mere usufruct.

[18] See Lucretius, *On the Nature of Things*, III, 960–975.

This argument assumes a particular representation of life as a good received in usufruct rather than in property.[19] By changing the representation of life, that argument modifies our view of death. If Man is not the owner of his lifetime, dying is not about being deprived on one's own lifetime: this is only about transmitting life—not *my* lifetime, but just lifetime, as a resource in usufruct—to next generations.

Note that the postulate stating that life is given in usufruct is not sufficient to imply the neutrality of death. One should 'leave the place', writes Lucretius. Here is the second postulate: a fixed quantity of lifetime would exist for all generations, past, present and future. Given this resource constraint, it is not fair, for a person, to benefit too long from the products of life, because other generations should also be able to benefit from these products. But this postulate raises also some questions: why does the fact of living longer prevents a younger person from living her own life? This third argument of Lucretius raises as many questions as the previous ones.

2.3 Seneca and the Wasted Lifetime

In *On the Shortness of Life*, Seneca stresses that most humans regard their death as a kind of 'universal evil'. However, that view is, according to Seneca, erroneous. The problem does not lie in an insufficiently long life, but, instead, in *what Man does with the lifetime he can enjoy*. Life has been given to humans, but they do not make a good use of it[20]:

> It's not that we have a short time to live, but that we waste much of it. Life is long enough, and it's been given to us in generous measure for accomplishing the greatest things, if the whole of it is well invested. But when life is squandered through soft and careless living, and when it's spent on no worthwhile pursuit, death finally presses and we realize that the life which we didn't notice passing has passed away.

[19] The usufruct is a jurisprudence term that designs the enjoyment of the revenues of a good, whose property belongs to another person. Being usufructuary of life—rather than the owner of his life—means that enjoying the products to which existence gives access, without considering oneself as the owner of one's life.

[20] See Seneca, *On the Shortness of Life*, I, 3.

To the men who complain about being simple mortal beings, Seneca replies that their life is sufficiently long, but that Man makes his own life short: ‘So it is: the life we are given isn’t short but we make it so; we’re not ill provided but we are wasteful of life’.[21] Seneca denounces a *waste* of lifetime. It is that waste—and not death—that makes life short, too short. The length of a life is not determined by the quantity of life-time that is available, but by what the person does with that quantity of time. A wasted life is necessarily short, whatever the age at death is.

According to Seneca, the waste of lifetime has its roots in the *immaterial* nature of that resource. This particular feature of lifetime makes humans forget about it being scarce. Seneca dedicates his essay to the description of various manners through which humans waste their (scare) lifetime. One of the major obstacles to life consists in being permanently suspended to the future. This attitude tends to spoil present times and to sacrifice these on the altar of the future: ‘They lose the day in looking forward to the night, the night in fear of the dawn’.[22] Another waste of time consists in being invested in occupations, the person being perpetually suspended to other persons. But Seneca mentions also other causes of wasting time, such as the false idleness (activity aimed at doing nothing), the quest for a social reputation (often acquired at the cost of living one’s life) and useless erudition (the search for the ‘first man’ who did some particular thing).

What would a non-wasted life look like? Seneca states that the only persons who really live their life are these who spend their time while looking for wisdom. Wisdom allows individuals to adopt a right attitude towards all moments of their life. Embracing the past through one’s memories, living the present fully and anticipating the future without fear: here is the key for a complete life, in opposition to the short life of persons suspended to the future.

By neglecting the quest for wisdom, humans tend to waste the limited quantity of lifetime they have. A corollary of this—human-made—shortness of life is the neutrality of death. According to Seneca, existing a few more years is not synonymous of living longer. Life, when it is wasted, remains short, whatever the length of existence is[23]:

[21] See Seneca, *On the Shortness of Life*, I, 4.

[22] See Seneca, *On the Shortness of Life*, XVI, 5.

[23] See Seneca, *On the Shortness of Life*, VII, 10.

> So there's no reason to believe that someone has lived long because he has grey hair and wrinkles: he's not lived long but long existed. For suppose you thought that a person had sailed far who'd been caught in a savage storm as soon as he left harbour, and after being carried in this direction and that, was driven in circles over the same course by alternations of the winds raging from different quarters: he didn't have a long voyage, but he was long tossed about.

From Seneca's point of view, a premature death is not an evil: what a death interrupts, it is not, to retain the cruise metaphor, an exploration full of discoveries, but, rather, an unfinishable round tour at the entrance of the harbour. The tendency of humans to waste their lifetime makes all lives short, whatever the effective duration of existence is.

What should we think about this neutrality thesis? Seneca's argument relies on the idea of a waste of lifetime. The waste of time is so generalized that it makes the length of lives—and, hence, the event of a premature death—almost anecdotal. However, the notion of a wasted life is questionable, since it is not easy to see how one can draw the frontier separating, in an objective way, activities that are worth being pursued from other activities. Who should be in charge of drawing that boundary? Liberal theories of social justice—following Rawls—defend that the persons themselves are the ones who should define their own conception of the good life.[24] In that way, liberal theories of justice are in opposition with the perfectionist approach defended by Seneca. On their side, welfare economists have also adopted the idea that individual preferences should be respected. From that perspective, it is out of question to talk about the waste of lifetime.[25]

2.4 Wittgenstein and the Intemporal Life

It is at the end of his *Tractatus Logico-Philosophicus* that Wittgenstein considers the issue of death, probably in order to clarify the meaning of some propositions about life and death[26]:

[24] See Rawls (1971).

[25] One exception could arise in the case of a coordination failure in time allocation leading to a socially suboptimal equilibrium. But this is not the kind of argument that Seneca had in mind when he underlined Man's tendency to waste time.

[26] See Wittgenstein (1922, 6.4311).

> Death is not an event of life. Death is not lived through. If by eternity is understood not endless temporal duration but timelessness, then he lives eternally who lives in the present. Our life is endless in the way that our visual field is without limit.

This passage of the *Tractatus* tells us things about what death is. First of all, Wittgenstein localizes the event of the death of a person outside the life of that person (in line with the second argument developed by Epicurus). Then, Wittgenstein argues that it is possible to reach eternity, in the sense not of immortality, but of a kind of intemporality (being out of time). A life fully anchored in the present has, according to Wittgenstein, no temporal boundaries, no limit. That second point tends to qualify the relevancy of the length of life.

Living entirely in the present—without considering the past or the future—protects individuals against troubles related to life and death. Being immerged in the present prevents the persons from regretting things lived (or not) in the past and preserves them also from the regrets caused by a life that would seem to be too short. Moreover, a total immersion in the present immunizes persons against all expectations and hopes related to the future—and the suspension to the future criticized by Seneca—and, by doing so, this protects also the persons against the regrets due to non-realized projects in the future in case of premature death. If one assumes that the intemporality of life makes the duration of existence secondary, it follows that death is (almost) neutralized: it is not a primary cause of harm for the deceased.

Wittgenstein proposes here some conditions for the—possible—neutrality of death: eternity could be achieved by living fully in present times, without worrying about the past or the future. But this position raises nonetheless some questions. Does a full immersion in the present make the length of life—and, hence, death—neutral, or does it contribute only to make a death a bit less damageable than it would otherwise be? And if an intemporal life neutralizes death, is it still possible to evaluate a life as a whole, to tell things about the goodness or the badness of lives taken entirely (and not just about their temporal parts)? We will re-examine these issues later on in this chapter.

2.5 Bachelard and the Fabric of Duration

In *L'intuition de l'instant*, Gaston Bachelard states, in opposition to Henri Bergson, that the real substance of time does not consist in durations, but in instants. According to Bergson, instants are just the product of human abstraction. On the contrary, Bachelard argues that durations are a human construct[27]:

> Time is noticed solely through instants; duration – we shall soon see how – is felt solely through instants. Duration is a dust cloud of instants or, better yet, a group of points organized more or less coherently by a phenomenon of perspective. Our need to descend all the way down to temporal points without individual dimension is now evident. For the line that connects the dots and schematizes duration is no more than a panoramic and retrospective function, the indirectly subjective and secondary nature of which we will demonstrate in what follows.

The primary component of time is the instant, and it is by a mental construction that durations are brought to existence. The existence of durations is as fragile as it is temporary. As Bachelard underlines when evoking the functioning of memory: 'Memory, that guardian of time, guards the instant alone. It preserves nothing, absolutely nothing, of our complicated and artificial sense of duration'.[28]

The conception of time as composed primarily of instants—and not of durations—implies several corollaries for the representation of the individual across time, that is, for what one calls the identity of a person. Durations exist only as the outcome of a production process, and persons use habits and life routines in order to create their identity as individuals.

More precisely, the intertemporal human being is, according to Bachelard, only an accidental sum of elements, a composition that takes the form of a life only through a perspective effect, in the same way as a set of close dots ends up representing a line in a space. The identity that the individual constructs—the permanency that he creates for himself—realizes itself by 'copying today on yesterday'. Habits and life routines make the impression of continuity possible and make the person conceive his

[27] See Bachelard (1931), English version (2013, p. 20).

[28] See Bachelard (1931), English version (2013, p. 21).

life. The real age of a person is the age of her life routines: 'Our arteries bear the age of our habits'.

This representation of life is not without consequence for the conception of death and the related harms. The duration of a life being a construct, what a death interrupts is conditional on the underlying construction. If a person lives while meticulously copying her past, her death interrupts a long life, which could have been lengthened further by the strength of life habits. If, on the contrary, life routines are absent, the past life has no duration: this is just a series of disordered instants, exactly as scattered points in space. In that case, death does not interrupt a life: it only brings a series of disconnected instants to an end. The consequences of a death are thus relative to the duration that it interrupts and, hence, relative to the strength of habits through which a person created her temporal permanence, her life.

In *La dialectique de la durée*, Bachelard's analysis of the *consolidés de succession* goes beyond the analysis of the production of life duration, in order to introduce a distinction between two dimensions of time. Besides the duration or length of a time, Bachelard evokes the question of the wealth or density of a time. Bachelard distinguishes between the *horizontal* time and the *vertical* time (i.e., the intensity of time)[29]:

> The idea of length of time is secondary. [...] There is even an inverse relation between the psychological length of a period of time and its fullness. The fuller time is the shorter it seems. This trite remark should be given prime importance in temporal psychology. It should be the basis of a key concept. The advantage would then be seen of referring to richness and density rather than to duration. It is through this concept of density that we can fully appreciate those regular, peaceful hours when our efforts have real rhythm, hours that give us the impression of normal time.

At the scale of a human life, the intensity of time matters as much—if not more—as the horizontal dimension of time. A life can be spread on a large segment of the horizontal axis of time while remaining close to the 0 level along the vertical axis of time.

If a life is like a poetic composition, how could one compose one's life in the most harmonious manner? Bachelard's answer is that a successful

[29] See Bachelard (1950), English version (2000, pp. 43–44).

life is a life 'made of well-ordered times'. In that perspective, a key dimension is *rhythm*, 'the only way of order and preserve diverse energies'. The rhythm, the 'basis for vital dynamics and psychical dynamics', consists of restoring, over time, a form. Rhythm is essential for the realization of a harmonious composition[30]:

> When life is successful, it is made of well-ordered times; vertically, it is made of superimposed and richly orchestrated instants; horizontally, it is linked to itself by the perfect cadence of successive instants that are unified in their role.

The just cadence of successive instants relies on a double requirement. On the one hand, a life made of well-ordered instants is a life that follows a rhythm in line with nature's own rhythms. One should thus avoid to living out of time. On the other hand, a successful life should be ordered according to a personal rhythm and not according to rhythms that come from outside. In order to have a successful life, one should make his life rhythmed in line with the rhythms of one's youth, the rhythms that favoured one's growth.

In sum, according to Bachelard, a life is like a poetic composition. What death interrupts—and the resulting harm—depends on the particular form of that composition. The emphasis laid by Bachelard on the vertical dimension of time (the intensity of time) allows to sketching out the conditions of a possible neutrality of death, by substitution of the vertical time to the horizontal time: the wealth or density of time could make a short life as good as a long life. But the conditions for such neutrality are somewhat restrictive: everything else being equal (*ceteris paribus*, that is, for a given density of time), the shortening of a well-rhythmed life harms the person (because it deprives her from intense instants). The existence of a vertical time—in addition to a horizontal time—is thus not sufficient to imply the neutrality of death. This neutrality prevails only if the life of the person was just a succession of disordered instants, like a set of scattered points lost in the space. Death is then neutral, in the precise sense that it interrupts something that had no duration, and which could not have lasted more (in the absence of that death).

[30] See Bachelard (1950), English version (2000, p. 130).

2.6 Nagel and the Deprivation Account

In *Mortal Questions*, Thomas Nagel raises the question of whether the death of a person harms that person. According to Nagel, three obstacles must be overcome in order to be able to answer that question[31]:

> First, doubt may be raised whether *anything* can be bad for a man without being positively unpleasant to him: specifically, it may be doubted that there are any evils which consist merely in the deprivation or absence of possible goods, and which do not depend on someone's *minding* that deprivation. Second, there are special difficulties, in the case of death, about how the supposed misfortune is to be assigned to a subject at all. There is doubt both as to *who* its subject is, and as to *when* he undergoes it. So long as a person exists, he has not yet died, and once he has died, he no longer exists; so there seems to be no time when death, if it is a misfortune, can be ascribed to its unfortunate subject. The third type of difficulty concerns the asymmetry, mentioned above, between our attitudes to posthumous and pre-natal non-existence. How can the former be bad if the latter is not?

The first two difficulties concern, respectively, the two arguments formulated by Epicurus, whereas the third difficulty is related to the symmetry argument developed by Lucretius. Let us examine how Nagel tackles these difficulties and brings the proof that *death is not neutral*, contrary to the theses defended by Epicurus and Lucretius.

Nagel overcomes the first difficulty by showing that the good and the bad are not reducible to sensations, unlike what Epicurus postulated. There exist several events that deteriorate the situation of a person *even though that person has no consciousness of being made worse-off*. Let us take the example, studied by Nagel, of a person who is mocked by his friends behind his back.[32] These mockeries taking place behind his back; the person has no consciousness of these nasty acts. But her situation would be better in the absence of these acts. Hence, we can say that these mockeries constitute a bad for the person.

One could reply to Nagel that this first example illustrates a form of lack of consciousness that is limited in comparison with the absence of consciousness in case of a death. Therefore, Nagel uses a second example,

[31] See Nagel (1979, p. 4).

[32] See Nagel (1979, p. 4).

the one of a young intelligent man who is victim of a brain attack, which reduces his level of intelligence to the one of a child.[33] The victim of that brain accident has no consciousness of his new mental condition. Thus, he cannot have any suffering from this. However, one can state that the brain accident did worsen the situation of the young intelligent man; that is, this event made him worse off. This second example, which involves a stronger degree of unconsciousness in comparison with the first one, illustrates, once again, that an event can worsen the situation of a person even when this has absolutely no consciousness of this deterioration.

Nagel completes his proof by a third example: the one of a person who dies prematurely, before the time where her children get married and have children themselves.[34] That person does not have the chance to see her family growing and flourishing. Like in the two preceding examples, the person has no consciousness of the worsening of her situation, because she is deceased. But, as in the two previous examples, it makes sense to say that her situation was deteriorated by the occurrence of that event.

The strength of Nagel's argument lies in the fact that if one accepts that, in the first two examples, the situation of the persons was worsened despite the absence of any awareness of this worsening, the epicurean premise of hedonism—i.e., the reduction of all goods and evils to mere sensations—vanishes: *there exist some events that are goods or evils for a person, even though this person is not conscious of these events*. The hedonistic premise being rejected, Epicurus's first argument cannot stand to critical analysis. Thus, one cannot justify the neutrality of death on the basis of the unconsciousness of the harm by the deceased. According to Nagel, the event of the premature death of a person deteriorates the situation of that person by depriving her of the goods she would have enjoyed provided that premature death did not take place. The fact that the deceased person is not conscious of being deprived does not suffice to make her death neutral. Despite the lack of consciousness, the deprivation caused by death exists, and death is bad precisely because it deprives the person of some goods that would have been enjoyed in the absence of death.

To this, an Epicurean thinker could reply that it is indeed the case that in Nagel's first example the situation of the person is deteriorated, but not in the two other examples. Actually, there exists a major difference

[33] See Nagel (1979, p. 5).

[34] See Nagel (1979, p. 7).

between the first example and the two other ones. In the first example, the person who is victim of a harm exhibits a stable form (i.e., remains the same person with or without the harm), whereas in the two other cases, the person who is the victim of a harm does no longer remain the person she was before the harm: she has changed (the young intelligent man has disappeared) or she died (third example).

This leads us to the second difficulty considered by Nagel: how can an event—and the associated harm—affect a person who is *not there any longer* at the time when the event occurs? Epicurus argued that the temporal localization of the event 'death' was outside the life of the person, so that this person could not be concerned by the event of her death.

Nagel considers, on the contrary, that some events can constitute evils for persons even though these persons are not present any longer when these events take place. Although the life of a person can be localized in time and space, this is not necessarily true for the (mis)fortunes that are assigned to her.[35] It would be too reductive to restrict the harms undergone by a person to these whose temporal location is clearly defined and lies within the period of existence of that person.

To illustrate that point, let us turn back to Nagel's second example. After the brain accident, the young intelligent person does not exist any longer, and one cannot pity the person that we can see now, because that new person has, strictly speaking, suffered from no harm. However, one can imagine what the young intelligent person *would have lived in the absence of the brain accident*, and, then, conceive that this person was definitely harmed by the brain attack. The temporal location of the harm is indeterminate. But the harm can be attached to the life of the young intelligent person.

This rationale can also be applied to the third example used by Nagel, that is, the existence of a harm caused by a premature death. Against Epicurus's second argument, Nagel argues that the absence of temporal overlapping between an event—the death—and the existence of a person

[35] See Nagel (1979, p. 5). Kamm (1993) criticized that view: if some post-mortem events can improve the overall situation of a deceased person (her life being taken as a whole), it is possible, for instance by improving the deceased's post-mortem reputation, to make her death less bad, thus reducing the harm caused by a premature death. However, one should notice that such post-mortem interventions could only have minor effects, and could hardly make death neutral.

is not a problem to qualify the badness of that event, because there exists no reason to restrict the set of harms underwent by a person to the subset of harms that can be temporally localized at times when that person exists. The question of the temporal location of an event is neither relevant, nor decisive to determine the existence or non-existence of a harm.[36]

Nagel overcomes this second difficulty by stating that nothing forces us to restrict the set of all events that are bad to a person to the subset of events that take place at times when this person still exists. As a consequence, a death can be considered as a one-off event, but that globally worsens the situation of the person who is deceased, her life being taken as a whole. This conclusion tends to question the plausibility of Epicurus's second argument. All in all, the premature death of a person is bad for her because of the deprivation due to that premature death, that is, because the death deprives the person from goods that would have been enjoyed in the absence of that event. The fact that the event of the death makes the person not exist any longer is not sufficient to make her death neutral, since one can reasonably imagine what the person would have been and would have lived in the hypothetical case of the absence of her death, and, hence, imagine the scope of the deprivation caused by death.

Let us now consider the third difficulty: the asymmetry in our attitudes concerning prenatal non-existence and post-mortem non-existence. What does Nagel reply to the symmetry argument? Nagel states that there exists a temporal asymmetry between what precedes the life of a person and what follows the life of that person. This asymmetry is due to the fact that the time preceding the birth of a person is not relevant for this person (since this person would have been another person in the hypothetical case of an earlier birth), whereas the time occurring after the death is relevant[37]:

> It is true that both the time before a man's birth and the time after his death are times when he does not exist. But the time after his death is time of which his death deprives him. It is time in which, had he not died then, he would be alive. Therefore any death entails the loss of some life that its victim would have led had he not died at that or any earlier point.

[36] That view was criticized by Bradley (2009), who considers that the temporal location of a harm is a necessary condition for the existence of that harm, contrary to Nagel's position.

[37] See Nagel (1979, p. 7).

> We know perfectly well what it would be for him to have had it instead of losing it, and there is no difficulty in identifying the loser.

A person who dies earlier than anticipated undergoes a loss, whose size depends on what she would have been able to live provided she did not die so early. Hence, there exists, in the case of a premature death, a harm. But one cannot, according to Nagel, say the same thing in case of a later birth. If a person were born earlier, she would just be a different person, and thus, she would not have won anything from being born earlier. Thus, a late birth does not deprive the person of any lifetime.

According to Nagel, whereas postponing the death of a person can save some extra lifetime for this person, advancing her birth would not contribute to give her extra lifetime, but would only modify her identity. This asymmetry between prenatal non-existence and post-mortem non-existence makes Nagel reject the symmetry postulate. Once again, the proof of the neutrality of death thesis vanishes, because of a premise that turns out to be, at the end of the day, questionable.[38]

2.7 Parfit's Patient

The symmetry argument is also criticized by Derek Parfit in *Reasons and Persons*, but for reasons that are distinct from the ones invoked by Nagel[39]:

> Let us first consider the argument with which Epicurus claimed that our future non-existence cannot be something to regret. We do not regret our past non-existence. Since this is so, why should we regret our future non-existence? If we regard one with equanimity, should we not extend this attitude to the other? Some claims that this argument fails because, while we might live longer, we could not have been born earlier. This is not a good objection. When they learnt that the square root of two was not a rational number, the Pythagoreans regretted this. We can regret truths even when it is logically impossible that these truths be false.

[38] Other criticisms against the symmetry argument were developed in the literature. Kamm (1993) argues that, even if a later birth and an earlier death both deprive a person from good things in life, two major differences exist between prenatal non-existence and post-mortem non-existence: the insulting nature of death (insult factor) and the fact that a death brings a life definitely to its end (extinction factor).

[39] See Parfit (1984, p. 175).

Parfit argues that the impossibility to be born earlier while keeping one's own identity is not sufficient to refute the symmetry argument.[40] However, according to Parfit, there exists another reason to reject the symmetry argument, and that reason consists of the existence of a bias towards the future. Human beings do not consider in the same manner all temporal parts of their life: they assign a larger weight to the future than to the past. This bias of humans in favour of the future explains why the symmetry argument does not succeed in establishing the neutrality of death.

In order to illustrate the existence of a bias towards the future, Parfit uses the example of a patient who sits in a recovery room, but does not know whether he had already the surgery or not (the so-called Surgery Case)[41]:

> I am in some hospital, to have some kind of surgery. Since this is completely safe, and always successful, I have no fears about the effects. The surgery may be brief, or it may instead take a long time. [...] Under a new policy, because the operation is so painful, patients are now afterwards made to forget it. Some drug removes their memories of the last few hours.
>
> I have just woken up. I cannot remember going to sleep. I ask my nurse if it has been decided when my operation is to be, and how long it must take. She says that she knows the facts about both me and another patient, but that she cannot remember which facts apply to whom. She can tell me only that the following is true. I may be the patient who had his operation yesterday. In that case, my operation was the longest ever performed, lasting ten hours. I may instead be the patient who is to have a short operation later today. It is either true that I did suffer for ten hours, or true that I shall suffer for one hour.
>
> I ask the nurse to find out which is true. While she is away, it is clear to me which I prefer to be true. If I learn that the first is true, I shall be greatly relieved.

[40] Note that Parfit seems here to assimilate the second argument proposed by Epicurus and the symmetry argument developed by Lucretius. In the rest of the text, he evokes Epicurus's argument which, for us, corresponds to the symmetry argument as proposed by Lucretius.

[41] See Parfit (1984, pp. 165–166).

The Surgery Case illustrates the existence of cognitive biases in favour of the future. If humans treated their past and their future in a symmetric manner, they would prefer having a painful surgery lasting one hour in the future rather than having a painful surgery lasting 10 hours in the past. However, as Parfit suggests, a majority of persons prefer having a long surgery in the past. This preference reveals that humans assign, in their assessment of lives, a more substantial weight to the future than to the past.

Let us now turn back to the evil of death. According to Parfit, the symmetry argument fails, because persons are biased towards the future. It could be the case that individuals regret their past non-existence. But the bias towards the future tends to reduce the relative importance of the past and to increase the weight assigned to the future[42]:

> Epicurus's argument therefore has force only for those people who both lack the bias towards the future, and do not regret their past non-existence. Since there are no such people, the argument has force for no one.

Parfit underlines that if humans were not biased towards the future, the approach of their death would be far less painful to them, and, as a consequence, they would be happier during their life.[43] For timeless individuals, the proximity of the event of death would matter less, because that event would be put on the same level as events lived by these persons in the past. The importance of death would then be qualified, to the largest benefit of humans themselves. The fear of death—the object of Epicurus and Lucretius's concerns—is exaggerated by the presence of a bias that prevents humans from considering all their life-periods with a similar interest.

2.8 Broome and the Intuition of Neutrality

Like Nagel and Parfit, John Broome rejects the thesis of the neutrality of death, but on different bases. Broome firstly notices that Epicurus's first argument relies on a particular conception of the good, hedonism,

[42] See Parfit (1984, p. 175).

[43] See Parfit (1984, pp. 176–177).

to which he does not adhere. Moreover, according to Broome, that argument assumes another postulate, which is also questionable[44]:

> So in pointing out that death deprives you of sensations, Epicurus goes no way towards showing it does not harm you. This is so even if we grant him hedonism as a premise. Hedonism has no tendency to suggest that death does not harm us. Epicurus forgets that the idea of harming involves a comparison. To harm someone you do not need to do something that is absolutely bad for her, whatever 'absolutely bad' might mean. You only need to make her less well off than she would otherwise have been. Death can have that effect.

According to Broome, any good or bad is *relative*: to say that an event is good amounts to say that this event is *better* than other events, so that goodness is reducible to betterness.[45] But since a good and a bad are relative to available alternatives, death can cause harm even in the absence of any post-mortem sensations, simply by preventing pleasant sensations from taking place. The absence of sensations after death is thus not sufficient to establish that death is neutral.

Then, Broome revisits the second argument proposed by Epicurus and questions the premises on which this relies. Broome asks: if an event is bad for a person, must there necessarily exist a time when that person suffers from that bad? Broome's answer is: No. The death of a person is precisely an event that contributes to worsen her situation without making that person suffer at any point in her life[46]:

> There is an obvious way for an event to harm you without harming you at any time: it only has to shorten your life.

According to Broome, Epicurus's arguments fail at establishing that death is necessarily neutral. But one can consider that what Epicurus wanted to defend is not that death is neutral, but, only, that humans should not worry about it, since one should only worry about the sole events that make a person suffer at some moments of her life[47]:

[44] See Broome (2004, pp. 236–237).

[45] See Broome (1999).

[46] See Broome (2004, p. 237).

[47] See Broome (2004, p. 238).

> When he [Epicurus] says 'Death is nothing to us', he may not mean death does not harm us. He may mean instead that we should not mind about dying. Perhaps we should not care about some of the harms we suffer, and perhaps the harm done by dying is one of those. Dying may harm you by making your life as a whole less good than it would have been had you lived longer. But perhaps you should not care about your life as a whole. Instead, perhaps you should care only about things that benefit or harm you at some time. Since death does not harm you at any time, then you should not mind about dying. Perhaps this is Epicurus's point.

If Broome's interpretation is correct, Epicurus's arguments should not be interpreted as proofs aimed at demonstrating the neutrality of death, but only as arguments aimed at convincing humans not to worry about their death (despite the badness of death).

Broome revisits also Wittgenstein's position relative to the eternal life. Wittgenstein recommends to 'live in the present', which amounts to worry only about the present and about nothing else. In that case, it is useless to worry about one's death, since this belongs to the future. Broome argues that worrying only about the present time—and ignoring any future perspective—could make a person imprudent and make her live constantly in a state of hunger, thirst and suffering. But such an interpretation could be too restrictive according to Broome. Actually, it could be that Wittgenstein recommends living in the present, while worrying about the future in the same way as one could worry about the good of other persons. Under that alternative interpretation, should we fear about death?

To that question, Broome brings a possible answer. A person living in the present could consider her future life *as a life lived by another, distinct person*, a new person who will be born in the future. From that perspective, a person could be indifferent with respect to her future death. Indeed, that person could not value the existence of another person in the future. And if the existence of that new person consists in the continuation of her own life, there could be indifference with respect to the duration of her future life and, hence, indifference with respect to the time of one's death.

But Broome rejects such an interpretation. The reason is that this interpretation would support the intuition of neutrality, which is, according to Broome, hardly plausible. The intuition of neutrality is the idea that adding or subtracting lives—or life-years—would have a neutral effect on social welfare. Broome rejects that intuition, by showing that this can lead to contradictions with basic intuitive principles. To illustrate that point, let us consider the following 4 lives. Lives A and D last one period (the symbol Ω represents the absence of life), whereas lives B and C last two periods[48]:

$$\text{Life A} = \{4, \Omega\} \ \text{Life B} = \{6, 1\}$$
$$\text{Life C} = \{4, 4\} \ \text{Life D} = \{6, \Omega\}$$

The intuition of neutrality recommends indifference between lives A and C, and between lives B and D. It seems also plausible that life D is strictly better than life A (because period well-being is larger in A than in B). Life D being strictly better than life A, and life A being as good as life C, one can obtain, by transitivity, that life D is strictly better than life C. But life C is strictly better than life B (because aggregate well-being is larger in C than in B), which, by transitivity, implies that life C is strictly better than life D. We reach here a contradiction: it cannot be true that life D is strictly better than life C and life C is strictly better than life D.

This example illustrates that the intuition of neutrality can lead to contradictions with other plausible principles (such as the transitivity of the betterness relation or the principle according to which, for an equal length, a life with a higher aggregate well-being is better than a life with a lower aggregate well-being). The intuition of neutrality should thus be abandoned and cannot be used to justify indifference with respect to death.

The only manner to justify indifference with respect to death is to use Wittgenstein's suggestion and to consider that one should not worry about one's entire life, but, *only, about the different parts of one's life*. This consists of adopting the interpretation of Epicurus's arguments provided by Broome: we should worry only about events that improve or deteriorate our life at some moments of our life. If such an attitude is adopted, there exists no contradiction in our example any more: since the person does not consider his life entirely, life C is no longer regarded as strictly better than life B, which allows us to avoid the contradiction. Thus focusing only on events that affect our well-being at a given point in our life can help us justifying that 'death is nothing to us'.

[48] Numbers indicate levels of utility per period.

But why should we concentrate only on the events that influence our well-being at different periods of life, and leave aside any interest for aggregate well-being defined along an entire life? Philosophers such as Broome, McMahan or Bradley—and welfare economists working on life and death issues—reject that position.[49] They consider that sacrificing all statements about the goodness or the badness of a life taken as a whole is a too large price to pay in order to rescue the thesis of the neutrality of death. They argue that death is, under general conditions, the source of deprivation and harm for the deceased person. The harm can be quantified by comparing two levels of well-being over the life cycle: on the one hand, the *effective* lifetime well-being, that is, the level of well-being associated with the life that the person actually lived; on the other hand, the lifetime well-being that would have been achieved in the *hypothetical* case of the absence of premature death. The gap between these two levels of lifetime well-being quantifies the harm caused by a premature death.[50]

2.9 Death Matters for Us

Let us turn back to the questions raised at the very beginning of this chapter. Does there exist a harm caused by a short life? Does a person who dies prematurely suffer from a loss? If yes, what are the determinants of the evil of death?

During Antiquity, Epicurus, Lucretius and Seneca argued—but for diverse reasons—that death is neutral. However, as we have seen, their arguments were based on some premises—such as hedonism or life satiation—that do not stand up to critical analysis. Regarding the representations of life proposed by Wittgenstein and Bachelard, these do not allow to justify the neutrality of death. These positions can be used to make appear the conditions of a possible neutrality of death or, more modestly, conditions making the quantity of lifetime secondary with respect to the intensity of lifetime, thought either as an anchoring in the present (Wittgenstein) or as a vertical time (Bachelard). At the end of the day, the thesis of the neutrality of death requires to give up any thought

[49] See Broome (2004), McMahan (2002), and Bradley (2009). Regarding the works of welfare economists on life and death, see Fleurbaey and Ponthiere (2023).

[50] Note that there exists no unique way to measure the loss of well-being due to a premature death. Methods differ concerning, among other things, the weights to be assigned to the distinct lost life-years. See Broome (2004, pp. 248–251).

about the goodness or the badness of a life taken as a whole, and to focus only on the well-being associated with the different life-periods, taken one by one. Such a position is questionable. Can't we know anything about the goodness or the badness of a life taken as a whole? One can seriously doubt about this.

True, the event of the premature death of a person does not affect the level of well-being of the different periods lived by that person. But it nonetheless affects the overall situation of that person, in the precise sense that her life taken as a whole would probably have been better provided the event of her premature death did not take place. *A premature death can thus worsen the situation of a person, without affecting her well-being at any point in her life, just by making her life shorter, thus depriving her from various good things of life*.

This is precisely what happened to Eligio Pereisson, the young Italian who died prematurely in *Il Sogno di Una Cosa*. True, the young Pereisson did not have the sensation of being deprived of anything. But he was harmed by his premature death, because his life taken as a whole would have been probably better provided he did not die prematurely. The premature death of Eligio Pereisson deprived him of many good things of life—even though the dream that inhabited him remained vague—and the mere fact of being deprived of these good things constitutes a harm, even if that harm is invisible.

It is not simple to measure the harm caused by a premature death. A first source of difficulty arises from the fact that, based on the deprivation account, the harm caused by a premature death depends on the quantity and the quality of life-years that would have been lived in the hypothetical absence of premature death. Such things are unobservable. The quantification of the harm due to a premature death thus requires assuming some counterfactuals.[51] Difficulties arise also because of the plurality of the conceptions of a good life. This heterogeneity in representations and preferences leads to various valuations of what is being lost in the case of

[51] The only case where counterfactuals are not needed would be when the value of a life-year is universal, that is, independent from its quality. But the intuition of universality is rejected by Fleurbaey and Ponthiere (2022), on the grounds that this would conflict with basic intuitions about the valuation of life.

premature death.[52] But these measurement difficulties should not make us deny the existence of harm due to premature death. Death definitely matters for us.

References

Bachelard, Gaston. 1931. *L'intuition de l'instant*. Paris: Vrin, English version *The Intuition of the Instant*, translated by Eileen Rizo-Praton, 2000.

Bachelard, Gaston. 1938. *La formation de l'esprit scientifique*. Paris: Vrin.

Bachelard, Gaston. 1950. *La dialectique de la durée*. Paris: Presses Universitaires de France, English version *The Dialectics of Duration*, translated by Mary McAllester Jones, 2013.

Bradley, Ben. 2009. *Well-Being and Death*. Oxford: Oxford University Press.

Broome, John. 1999. *Ethics Out of Economics*. Cambridge: Cambridge University Press.

Broome, John. 2004. *Weighing Lives*. Oxford: Oxford University Press.

Fleurbaey, Marc, and Gregory Ponthiere. 2022. 'The Value of a Life-year and the Intuition of Universality'. *Journal of Ethics and Social Philosophy* 22: 355–381.

Fleurbaey, Marc, and Gregory Ponthiere. 2023. 'Measuring well-being and Lives Worth Living'. *Economic Theory*, forthcoming.

Kamm, Frances. 1993. *Morality, Mortality*, vol. 1. Oxford: Oxford University Press.

MacMahan, Jeff. 2002. *The Ethics of Killing: Problems at the Margin of Life*. Oxford: Oxford University Press.

Nagel, Thomas. 1979. *Mortal Questions*. Cambridge: Cambridge University Press.

Parfit, Derek. 1984. *Reasons and Persons*. Oxford: Oxford University Press.

Pasolini, Pier-Paolo. 1962. *Il Sogno di Una Cosa*. French version. Le rêve d'une chose, 1965.

Pigou, Arthur Cecil. 1920. *The Economics of Welfare*. London: Macmillan.

Ponthiere, Gregory. 2017. *Economie du vieillissement*. Paris: Editions La Découvert.

Rawls, John. 1971. *A Theory of Justice*. Cambridge: Harvard University Press.

Sen, Amartya. 1977. 'Rational Fools: A Critique of the Behavioural Foundations of Economic Theory'. *Philosophy and Public Affairs* 6: 317–344.

[52] On the measurement of the welfare loss due to a premature death in the context of heterogeneous preferences and conceptions of a life worth living, see Fleurbaey and Ponthiere (2023).

Warren, James. 2004. *Facing Death: Epicurus and His Critics*. Oxford: Oxford University Press.
Wittgenstein, Ludwig. 1922. *Tractatus Logico-Philosophicus*. New York: Kegan Paul.

CHAPTER 3

An Insurance Against a Short Life

Abstract The existence of harm due to premature death constitutes a necessary, but not a sufficient condition for justifying the construction of a social insurance against a premature death. A key issue is whether or not this new pillar of social protection can be justified as an instrument serving the ideal of social justice. This chapter examines the desirability of a social insurance against a short life from the perspective of various ethical frameworks. It is first argued that neither utilitarianism nor Rawls's *Theory of Justice* justifies the construction of a social insurance against a short life. However, it is possible to justify it on the grounds of Fleurbaey's Principle of Compensation, according to which well-being inequalities due to circumstances should be abolished by the welfare state. At first glance, compensation for a premature death appears impossible, because victims of a premature death cannot be identified ex ante (when they are still alive), and cannot be compensated ex post (when they are dead). However, it is possible to construct a social insurance against a premature death by adopting age-based statistical discrimination favouring the young. By reallocating 'good things of life' towards young ages, one can improve the situation of *all* young persons, who will necessary include the persons who will turn out to die prematurely in the future.

Keywords Utilitarianism · Rawls · Compensation · Premature death · Age-based statistical discrimination

G. Ponthiere, *Allocating Pensions to Younger People*,
https://doi.org/10.1007/978-3-031-24748-4_3

If the conclusions of the previous chapter are correct, persons who die prematurely are victims of a harm, even though this harm remains invisible. A premature death deprives the person from supplementary life-years that would have allowed her to accomplish life projects. The existence of that hidden cost of a premature death invites us to raise the question of the necessity, for a society, to repair the harm caused by a short life.

By repairing a harm, we mean the setting of public policies (for instance, monetary transfers) limiting the well-being loss due to the occurrence of the harm. Let us take the example of the loss of a job. A worker who is fired undergoes a loss of income, as well as a deterioration of his social status. Our societies have built an institutional device—the unemployment insurance—allowing to repairing, at least to some extent, the harm caused by the loss of a job. Thanks to the unemployment insurance (payment of contributions by workers aimed at funding allowances paid to the unemployed), the society does collectively some efforts in order to compensate the harm faced in case of a job loss.[1]

Do our societies bring reparation to the persons who are the victims of a premature death? More fundamentally, is it possible to repair the harm caused by a short life? If yes, would such compensation be justified?

In its current form, the public system of social insurance provides no reparation in case of a premature death. The modern welfare state involves four pillars: the insurance against the risk of job loss (unemployment allowances), the insurance against the risk of disease (covering health care costs), the insurance against the risk of fertility (children allowances) and the insurance against the risk of ageing (pension systems), while a fifth pillar—the insurance against long-term care risks—is being constructed progressively.[2]

There exists no social insurance against the risk of a short life. It is actually even worse: existing pension systems impose a double penalty to the persons who die prematurely. Actually, current pay-as-you-go pension

[1] Note that, in most cases, the insurance device is said to be incomplete, in the sense that there remains some welfare loss due to the occurrence of the harm. For instance, the unemployment allowance is not sufficient to make the well-being of the unemployed as high as what it would have been in the absence of job loss.

[2] The insurance against ageing protects individuals against the risk of living so long that all their savings would be insufficient to cover their needs during the old age. See Barr and Diamond (2003, 2008) and Cremer and Pestieau (2011). Insurance against old-age poverty is advantageous for persons who enjoy a long life, but is disadvantageous for the ones who have a short life.

systems require the payment of contributions from workers, which are then paid to retirees (long-lived persons). These contributions reduce the purchasing power of young adults, who include the persons who will turn out to die prematurely (before reaching retirement). In its current form, the welfare state tends thus to worsen—even more—the situation of the persons who die prematurely.

The regressive feature of existing pension systems has been widely documented.[3] Existing retirement systems have a tendency to redistribute resources from short-lived persons to long-lived persons, *against any logic of compensation*. The forced savings induced by existing retirement systems increase the losses due to a short life. Although basic insurance principles would recommend to transferring resources from good states of nature—a long life—to bad states of nature—a short life—existing retirement systems do the exact opposite.

Could we imagine another welfare state, which would insure citizens against the risk of a short life? This question matters only insofar as it is socially desirable to construct an insurance against a short life. This chapter will thus first study the social desirability of short-life insurance and, then, will examine the form this insurance device could take.

The existence of harm caused by a short life is not sufficient, per se, to justify reparation or compensation by means of an insurance device. A normative proposition—stating what should be—cannot, in good logic, be deduced from purely positive premises—stating what is.[4] In order to deduce, from the existence of harm due to a premature death, that public authorities should intervene to compensate the harm, one must include, in the argument, some premises about the good or the right.

The study of the normative justification of an insurance against a short life requires first to define more precisely what one means by social justice. In *Social Justice*, David Miller proposes a simple definition of social justice: it is about giving to each person what is due to her.[5] When

[3] See Bommier et al. (2006), which shows, on the basis of data from the *Echantillon inter-régimes des retraités*, that the premature mortality of poor persons contributes to annihilate between one quarter and one half of the redistribution carried out by means of income-differentiated replacement rates (i.e., ratios of monthly pension allowance divided by the monthly wage when being active). See also Coronado et al. (2011).

[4] On this, see Moore (1912).

[5] See Miller (1976, Chapter 1). Miller studies three distinct definitions of 'what is due to a person', in terms of her merits, her needs or her rights.

formulated in these terms, the question of the justification of an insurance against a premature death can be written as follows: ***what does the society owe to individuals who die prematurely?***

In order to examine the justification of compensating the harm suffered by short-lived persons, this chapter will consider different conceptions of social justice. We will begin our explorations by adopting a widespread conception of justice—the utilitarian approach—and, then, we will examine alternative approaches, based on other principles of justice.

3.1 Utilitarianism and Premature Deaths

Developed by Jeremy Bentham in the eighteenth century, utilitarianism is an ethical doctrine that relies on a unique principle: the principle of utility or the principle of 'the largest happiness for the largest number'.[6] The principle of utility recommends that any individual action, any public policy or any institution should be oriented towards the pursuit of a single goal: the maximization of the sum of individual utilities, which measure the well-being of the different members of the society.[7] Utilitarianism thus requires choosing actions, policies and institutions that lead to the highest aggregate social welfare.

Utilitarianism relies on three pillars: consequentialism, welfarism and sum-ranking. That doctrine is consequentialist: only the consequences of actions, policies and institutions matter. The intentions that governed these choices are considered to be irrelevant: the only things that matter in the calculus of pleasures and pains are the consequences of these choices. But utilitarianism does not focus on any kind of consequences: there is an exclusive focus on the consequences in terms of utility or welfare. The informational basis regarded as relevant for social evaluation consists only of individual utilities. This is the second pillar of utilitarianism: welfarism. Finally, the principle of utility evaluates actions on the basis of their consequences on the sum of individual utilities, an equal weight being assigned to the utility of each person in the calculus of pleasures and pains (the sum-ranking criterion).

[6] See Bentham (1789).

[7] The term 'utility' does not have here the standard meaning of 'usefulness'. Bentham chose the term 'utility' to refer to a measure of pleasures and pains. The utility of a person in a particular situation is supposed to take into account all potential sources of pleasures and pains: consumption of goods and services, leisure time, health, etc.

How does utilitarianism treat the persons who turn out to die prematurely and have thus a short life? Given that utilitarianism consists of a calculus of pleasures and pains, one cannot answer that question without adding a few assumptions about the determinants of individual utilities aggregated in the utilitarian formula. For that purpose, let us assume that the utility over the entire life of a person is equal to the sum of temporal utilities for that person, that is, the utilities associated with the different periods of the life enjoyed by that person. Let us also assume, following Jevons, the law of diminishing marginal utility: a rise in consumption per period increases temporal utility over that period, but in an extent that decreases with the level of consumption over the period.[8]

Under these general hypotheses, it is possible to show that the principle of utility is far from giving priority, in the allocation of resources, to the short-lived. Actually, it is quite the opposite that takes place: utilitarianism tends, under these hypotheses, to favour the persons who have a long life, to the disadvantage of the persons who die prematurely. Thus, the application of the principle of utility tends generally to increase, in comparison with the laissez-faire (absence of public intervention), the size of the harm due to a premature death.

In order to illustrate that result, let us consider a simple resource allocation problem among two persons, named Kurt and Philomena, who share the same interests in life.[9] For the sake of simplification, these two persons have the same initial endowment of resources, which is allocated in equal shares among each period of their life. Let us suppose that Kurt has a short life, which lasts only one period (for instance, 40 years), whereas Philomena has a life that is twice longer (for instance, 80 years). How will a utilitarian government allocate the resource—e.g., a given amount of wealth—between these two persons?

Aggregate utility is maximized when transferring, at the margin, one euro from one use to another use does not change aggregate utility. This takes place when the utility gains associated with such a transfer are exactly equal to the utility losses generated by that transfer. The optimal allocation under utilitarianism is obtained when the marginal utilities of

[8] See Jevons (1871). The marginal utility of consumption is defined as the variation of utility induced by an infinitesimal change in consumption.

[9] Kurt and Philomena share the same utility function, which is the sum of temporal utilities along their life.

the different uses of the resource are equalized.[10] In our example, this equalization is achieved by distributing the income equally across the three life-periods considered: the unique life-period of Kurt and the two periods lived by Philomena. Utilitarianism justifies giving (twice) more resources to Philomena than to Kurt. The utilitarian government will thus use fiscal instruments to transfer one part of Kurt's initial endowment to Philomena, in line with what the principle of utility recommends. That example could be generalized to N persons.[11]

The principle of utility implies transferring resources from short-lived persons toward long-lived persons. The maximization of social welfare is achieved by allocating more resources to persons who enjoy longer lives. This result is explained by the stronger capacity of long-lived persons to transform resources into utility, in comparison with persons who have a short life.

Is such an allocation of resources, which favours the long-lived, in line with our basic intuitions about social justice? There are serious reasons to have doubts about this. The problem lies in the mere fact that utilitarianism, by transferring resources from short-lived persons towards long-lived persons, tends to increase the size of the harm caused by a premature death, against any idea of reparation or compensation.

This point is fundamental: although the lengths of life are, to a large extent, the outcome of Nature's lottery, this is not the same for the harms caused by short lives. The harm caused by a short life—i.e., the extent to which a premature death deprives the deceased persons—depends on how resources are being allocated along the human life cycle and, hence, also, on public policies that influence the intertemporal allocation of resources. The more the resources are concentrated at old ages, the larger the harms caused by a premature death are. To the extent that these affect the allocation of resources across ages of life, public policies influence the size of the harm caused by a premature death.[12]

[10] This can be shown by *reductio ad absurdum*. Let us consider the utilitarian optimum. If marginal utilities were not equal at that optimum, it would be possible, by transferring some euros from one person to another, to increase the aggregate sum of utilities. This would mean that the initial allocation is not the one that maximizes social welfare, that is, a contradiction.

[11] This result is true whatever the utilitarian government can or cannot anticipate the length of life of each person.

[12] We will reexamine that key point later on in this essay. This is precisely because the harm caused by a premature death depends on the intertemporal allocation of resources

3.2 The Limits of Utilitarianism

As we have just seen, the utilitarian social criterion recommends to transferring resources from the persons who die prematurely to the persons who live longer. By doing so, this ethical doctrine goes against the idea of reparation. When facing this kind of result, two attitudes are possible. On the one hand, one could be satisfied with this—somewhat disturbing—result. On the other hand, one can consider that the implications of utilitarianism in the context of unequal longevity are opposite to our moral intuitions, and, as such, tend to question the adequacy of the principle of utility as a criterion for social justice.

Out of these two options, the second one seems to be the most reasonable. Utilitarianism leads to unattractive implications in the context of inequalities in the length of life. The principle of utility has here implications that are opposite to our basic moral intuitions: the persons who die prematurely are penalized, and utilitarianism proposes nothing less than to impose a second penalty to these victims, by reallocating resources from short-lived persons to long-lived persons.

Although utilitarianism exhibits several appealing properties in the particular context of a society where all members are identical, its implications are far less attractive under heterogeneous populations, and, in particular, when individuals have unequal longevities.[13] The principle of utility does not provide satisfactory account of social justice in a world where individuals enjoy lives of unequal length, and, as such, should be given up.

This questioning of utilitarianism is based on the reflexive equilibrium method used by John Rawls in his *Theory of Justice*. That method consists of examining the foundations of an ethical doctrine by deducing all implications of that doctrine and, then, compares these implications with moral intuitions. In the case of unequal lifetimes, the implications of utilitarianism are so distant from basic intuitions that the reflexive equilibrium method requires departing from the principle of utility. Throughout the

along the life cycle that a system of reverse retirement—which concentrates consumption and leisure time at young ages rather than at older ages—can allow for a reduction of the size of the harm due to a premature death and, hence, can contribute to bring more social justice (see Chapter 4).

[13] On this point, see Mirrlees (1982).

rest of this essay, we will thus give up the principle of utility and consider alternative ethical criteria.

In our view, only one strategy could reconcile the implications of utilitarianism under unequal longevity with basic moral intuitions, but that strategy is itself subject to some questionings. Actually, one possible way to rescue utilitarianism in this context would consist of treating a person who lives different periods as *distinct persons*. In our example, this would consist of denying the existence of Philomena over two periods and considering that there exists one person, called Philomena 1, whose life lasts one period, and another person, called Philomena 2, who lives also one period. Under that alternative description of the allocation problem, the utilitarian solution looks more attractive: each distinct person—Kurt, Philomena 1 and Philomena 2—receives, under the principle of utility, the same amount of resources.

But that way of rescuing the principle of utility has a cost: this requires generalizing the occurrence of a premature death to *all* lives under consideration. Thus, the principle of utility would be rescued by making the mere idea of longevity inequalities vanish. Such a defence strategy is questionable: this chapter aims at thinking about social justice in the context of unequal lifetime and not at thinking about social justice while supposing that all individuals enjoy the same duration of life. One must thus give up the principle of utility.

3.3 Rawls and Lifetime Inequalities

In his *Theory of Justice*, John Rawls points to several major shortcomings of utilitarianism as a system of ethics. First of all, utilitarianism assumes full comparability of individual utilities among all members of the society. This is a strong postulate: individuals pursue various conceptions of the good life, and it is hard to put all these conceptions and the associated achievements along a common scale of value. Moreover, utilitarianism only assigns an instrumental value to fundamental liberties (i.e., they matter only insofar as they lead to the largest aggregate social welfare). Against that view, Rawls argues that several fundamental liberties should be defended for their own sake, independently of their consequences on social welfare. Finally, Rawls is also critical of the fact that, when individuals differ in their capacity to transform resources into utility, utilitarianism can justify quite unequal allocations of resources and, hence, unequal distributions of utilities across individuals (since only the maximization of the sum of utilities matters from a utilitarian perspective).

As a reaction to these limitations of utilitarianism, Rawls developed an alternative conception of social justice. In order to avoid the problem of incomparability of utilities across individuals, Rawls proposed to give up the metric of utilities and to make his theory of justice rely on another metric, which constitutes a more objective basis: primary goods. Primary goods are defined as resources necessary to pursue one's conception of the good life, whatever this is.[14] The second problem faced by utilitarianism is solved by relying on a specific criterion of distribution for the allocation of fundamental liberties within the society. The third limitation of utilitarianism is overcome by giving up the aggregative criterion of the sum (of utilities), in order to give a stronger weight to the most disadvantaged individuals.

Rawls's theory of justice involves three fundamental principles, which make it possible to evaluate and rank different institutions, according to their implications on the distribution of social primary goods. According to Rawls, these three principles of justice would be chosen by individuals put in the original position, that is, in a hypothetical situation where all individuals would be under a veil of ignorance and would thus abstract from their social position, their values, their skills, etc. The original position is a thought experiment that makes it possible to take into account impartiality constraints in the ethical deliberation. Without these constraints, individuals could be tempted to select principles of justice describing institutions favouring—in a partial way—the interests of some persons.

The three principles describing just institutions can be briefly presented as follows. First of all, the principle of equal liberty, which states that institutions should be designed in such a way that each person has equal right to the largest set of fundamental liberties generalizable to the society as a whole. Second, the principle of fair equality of opportunity: institutions should be such that socio-economic inequalities are associated with

[14] According to Rawls (p. 62), primary goods are 'things that every rational man is presumed to want'. Rawls adds: 'These goods normally have a use whatever a person's rational plan of life'. Primary goods include 'natural primary goods', which are not under the control of institutions (e.g. inherited health), and 'social primary goods', whose distribution is under the control of institutions. Social primary goods include fundamental liberties (freedom of speech, etc.), chances of access to social positions, income, wealth and bases of self-respect.

social positions to which all persons have equal chances of access, for a given skills level. Finally, the difference principle: socio-economic inequalities should be to the benefit of the most disadvantaged persons in the society.[15] Notice that the first principle of justice has priority over the second and the third principles, and that the second principle has priority over the third one.

Being designed as an alternative to utilitarianism, Rawls's theory of justice can avoid some major shortcomings of the utilitarian doctrine. But can we use Rawls's principles of justice to provide normative foundations for the reparation of harms due to a premature death?

As we shall see, Rawls's *Theory of Justice* does not allow us to justify the construction of a social insurance against the risk of a short life. Harms caused by a premature death are not regarded as relevant from a Rawlsian perspective and for two distinct reasons. On the one hand, the lifetime resource is not, *stricto* sensu, a primary good in the Rawlsian sense. On the other hand, the Rawlsian conception of justice focuses on *expectations* about life projects, rather than on the *effective* realization of these projects. This exclusive focus on expectations rather than realizations makes inequalities in realized longevity irrelevant from the perspective of realizing social justice. Let us now explain these two points further.

It should be underlined that human longevity is not mentioned by Rawls when he defines primary goods, these things that every rational man prefers to have in a larger quantity.[16] Does each rational man prefer *more* lifetime to *less* lifetime, whatever his life plans are? One can have doubts about this and consider that longevity itself is not a primary good. On the contrary, what might constitute a primary good is a kind of minimal longevity basis, rather than longevity itself. Indeed, everyone needs, in order to realize one's life plans, a minimum duration of existence, that is, a sufficiently long life. This minimal longevity basis could thus constitute a primary good in Rawls's sense of a thing that any rational man wants, whatever his conception of the good life is. Hence,

[15] Inequalities in income and wealth are justified only to the extent that these serve the interests of the most disadvantaged persons, i.e., only if the situation of these persons would be deteriorated in the absence of these inequalities. Thus, the difference principle tends to restrict substantially the domain of acceptable inequalities.

[16] See John Rawls, *A Theory of Justice*, Sects. 11 and 15. Notice that health is, unlike longevity, listed as a natural primary good (see Sect. 11).

from the perspective of Rawlsian social justice, inequalities in lifetime are not necessarily relevant: only the deprivation of a minimal longevity basis matters.[17]

But even if one treats a minimal longevity basis as a natural primary good, this does not, in my view, suffice to justify, on Rawlsian bases, the construction of a social insurance against the risk of a short life. Actually, according to Rawls, interpersonal comparisons should be made in terms of 'expectations of social primary goods'[18]:

> The difference principle also avoids difficulties by introducing a simplification for the basis of interpersonal comparisons. These comparisons are made in terms of expectations of primary social goods. In fact, I define these expectations simply as the index of these goods which a representative individual can look forward to. One man's expectations are greater than another's if this index for someone in his position is greater. Now primary goods, as I have already remarked, are things which it is supposed a rational man wants whatever else he wants. Regardless of what an individual's rational plans are in detail, it is assumed that there are various things which he would prefer more or rather than less. With more of these goods men can generally be assured of greater success in carrying out their intentions and in advancing their ends, whatever these ends may be.

Interpersonal comparisons of situations are made on the basis of expectations of primary social goods and not on the basis of the effective realization of life plans. Rawls is explicit on this precise point[19]:

> It may be objected that expectations should not be defined as an index of primary goods anyway but rather as the satisfactions to be expected when plans are executed using these goods. After all, it is in the fulfilment of these plans that men gain happiness, and therefore the estimate of expectations should not be founded on the available means. Justice as fairness, however, takes a different view. For it does not look behind the use which

[17] One could reply to this that if Rawls defines his index of social primary goods along the entire lifecycle, then longevity would enter the calculations indirectly, short-lived persons having in general less accumulated wealth along the lifecycle. True, but the problem is that under this definition of the index of social primary goods, short-lived very wealthy persons could be regarded as better off than long-lived individuals, a questionable view.

[18] See Rawls (1971, p. 92).

[19] See Rawls (1971, p. 94).

persons make of the rights and opportunities available to them in order to measure, much less to maximize, the satisfactions they achieve.

Harms due to a premature death are not relevant from a Rawlsian perspective, because these harms concern the effective non-realization of life plans, instead of expectations about the realization of life plans. When considering a person whose life is shortened by a premature death, one does not consider expectations about the realization of life goals, but realizations of life projects, i.e., what persons really achieve or not in their life. We are thus far from what a representative agent can expect to achieve given some available means.

In sum, according to Rawls, just institutions are the ones which provide to all citizens the *means* (liberties, income, wealth, etc.) that give them opportunities to realize their life plans. But social justice, in a Rawlsian perspective, stops there: it does not justify the reparation, ex post, of harms caused by accidents of life. This distinction is particularly relevant for the understanding of the Rawlsian treatment of the harm caused by a premature death. The Rawlsian approach to social justice thus does not allow us to provide a justification for the compensation of the harm caused by a short life.[20]

3.4 Responsibility and Compensation

But it is too early to conclude from all this that there exists no normative foundation to the construction of a social insurance against the risk of a short life. Bentham's utilitarian ethics and Rawls's liberal-egalitarian ethics are just two theoretical settings among a large number of approaches to social justice. One can find, among these other ethical approaches, theories that do justify the reparation of the harm caused by a premature death.

[20] This criticism is similar to the one made by Sen (1980) against Rawls's *Theory of Justice* in the light of the example of a handicapped person: by focusing on the distribution of means (primary goods)—and by ignoring heterogeneity in the capacity of humans to use these means in order to effectively meet their life-goals—the Rawlsian framework leaves some injustices uncompensated. Like the handicapped person, a short-lived person can also be described as a person who has more difficulties to convert means into her life-goals.

Let us consider the theory of responsibility and compensation developed by Marc Fleurbaey.[21] That theory of justice involves two fundamental principles. On the one hand, the principle of liberal reward, according to which well-being inequalities that result from variables controlled by individuals should be left unaffected by the state. On the other hand, the principle of compensation, according to which well-being inequalities due to pure circumstances should be abolished by the state. Together, these two principles defend the view that what matters for social justice is not so much the extent of inequalities, than the origin of these inequalities. Some inequalities are the outcome of individual decisions, and it is just that the persons who took decisions leading to these inequalities are taken as responsible for these inequalities. However, when inequalities are due to circumstances, i.e., variables that lie outside any individual control, victims of these inequalities should not be regarded as responsible for their situation. A corrective intervention by the state is then justified, in order to neutralize the effects of circumstances on individual outcomes.

Unfortunately, as this was stressed by Fleurbaey, these two principles of justice—the principle of liberal reward and the principle of compensation—have contradictory implications. The problem lies in the fact that in many real-life situations, individual outcomes are the product of interactions between pure circumstances and choice variables (e.g., efforts). In such cases, it is not possible, by a redistributive policy, to neutralize inequalities due to circumstances while, at the same time, leave inequalities caused by choice variables unaffected. One of the two principles must be abandoned to the benefit of the other.

That negative result matters for the issue at stake here, because the harm caused by a premature death is determined both by circumstances and by choice variables.

Actually, the demographic literature on the causes of longevity inequalities shows that lifetime inequalities are the output of various interacting causes, of distinct natures. Whereas some causes—such as the genetic background—are pure circumstances, other causes—such as lifestyles—seem to be under the responsibility of the persons, even if the adoption of lifestyles is dependent on the surrounding social environment to which

[21] See Fleurbaey (2009).

one belongs (including the family), which looks also, to some extent, like a circumstance.[22]

The harm caused by a short life depends on circumstances, such as the type of mandatory retirement system that prevails (including the size of mandatory contributions to pension systems), but also on individual decisions, such as savings decisions. Actually, a young person who saves for his old days loses more in case of a premature death, in comparison with a person who did not save a lot. Lost resources—and thus welfare losses too—are larger the higher savings is: higher saved amounts imply, *ceteris paribus*, lower consumption when the young person was still alive, and, thus, a more severe deprivation in case of early death.[23]

Given that circumstances and choice variables jointly determine the harm caused by a premature death, a distributive policy cannot satisfy both the principle of compensation and the principle of liberal reward. But which of these two principles should we keep to give an account of social justice?

Throughout this chapter, we will keep the principle of compensation and leave the principle of liberal reward aside. Note that the reflexive equilibrium method used above does not allow us to justify our adoption of the principle of compensation rather than the principle of liberal reward, since both principles can, in some contexts, lead to implications contrary to moral intuitions, thus inviting revision of these principles. The principle of liberal reward has the unattractive implication of considering extreme inequalities as fair, as long as these follow from individual decisions. Regarding the principle of compensation, it can also imply some counter-intuitive implications, for instance when the neutralization of inequalities due to circumstances implies a 'levelling down' of the situations of all persons.

[22] On the influence of the genetic background, Christensen et al. (2006) show, by means of comparisons of lengths of life among pairs of monozygotic and dizygotic twins, that about 25–33% of longevity inequalities within a cohort are due to the genetic background. Regarding the effect of lifestyles, see Balia and Jones (2008). They show that about 25% of longevity inequalities are due to lifestyles (alcohol, tobacco, physical activity, sleeping patterns).

[23] Note that in the presence of altruism, the transmission—through bequests—of lost savings to siblings can reduce, to some extent, the harm caused by a premature death, but only to some extent.

Although the reflexive equilibrium method cannot allow us to select one principle out of these, it is nonetheless possible to justify our adherence to the principle of compensation rather than the principle of liberal reward by using another method of justification, known as the *prior principle* method.[24] That method justifies a principle by demonstrating that this principle can be deduced from a primary, i.e., more fundamental, principle. For that purpose, let us turn back to Miller's definition of social justice as 'to each according to one's due'. Among the possible definitions of what is due to a person, the one that seems the most attractive to us is 'to give to each person according to her needs'.[25] If one adopts that view of justice, the principle of liberal reward must be rejected, because distributions resulting from individual choices are often far away from distributions according to the needs. However, the principle of compensation can find a more solid justification here: compensating individuals for circumstances amounts, in a large class of cases, to give more resources to the persons who have the most urgent needs, in line with the prior principle.[26] Hence, if 'to each according to one's needs' is taken as a prior principle of justice, the prior principle method provides more solid foundations for the principle of compensation.

Let us turn back to longevity inequalities. If one adopts a complete life view, the persons who die prematurely have stronger needs for enjoying good things in their (short) life, in comparison with individuals who have longer lives. These more urgent needs of the short-lived justify a compensation for the persons who die prematurely.

Adopting the principle of compensation has thus important implications in the context of unequal longevities: if one assumes that the harm due to a premature death is mainly due to circumstances, this principle justifies an intervention of the state, in such a way as to repair the harm

[24] See Sen (1980).

[25] This conception of social justice 'to each according to one's needs' was evoked by Marx (1875) in his *Critique of the Gotha Program*: 'from each according to his abilities, to each according to his needs'.

[26] It should be stressed that one can find some particular situations where the principle of compensation has implications that are opposite to the ones of the principle of distribution according to needs. Thus, the prior principle method does not allow us to provide an absolute support for the principle of compensation, but, rather, to say that for a broad class of situations, the principle of compensation is more in line with the principle of justice based on needs, rather than the principle of liberal reward.

caused by a premature death, precisely on the ground of compensating the victims of a short life for the harm they suffer. The principle of compensation thus allows us to justify the compensation of the harm caused by a premature death.

But how could one repair the harms caused by an early death? Answering that question requires to resolving the problem raised by the compensation of persons who die prematurely. In the following pages, we will explore the construction of what we could call a social insurance against the risk of having a short life.

3.5 Is an Insurance Against a Short Life Possible?

Can one construct an insurance against a premature death, while following a structure close to the one of existing social insurance devices, such as the social health insurance or the unemployment insurance?

Without any doubt, the answer is: No, because of a simple reason: the harm suffered in case of a death is singular and much different from the harm due to a disease or a job loss. Before examining the conditions under which some social short-life insurance can be constructed, let us first highlight two major difficulties raised by the compensation of the harm due to a premature death.[27]

First of all, persons who die prematurely are, by definition, not alive any longer once the event of their premature death has taken place. As a consequence, it is extremely difficult, after their death, to improve their situation in any way. We face here a fundamental difference with respect to the construction of other social insurance systems. These other, existing social insurance devices concern events that leave the victims alive, so that some repairing or corrective intervention (e.g., a monetary compensation) is possible after the occurrence of the event causing harm. For instance, in the case of the loss of a job, the state can intervene after the job loss took place, in order to compensate the worker who lost his job, for instance by paying to him an unemployment allowance. Unfortunately, this type of ex post compensation (after the occurrence of the

[27] On these difficulties, see Fleurbaey et al. (2014).

harm) is extremely difficult to carry out in case of a premature death. The state cannot improve, ex post, the situation of the persons who were made worse off by a premature death, simply because these persons are dead.[28]

A second difficulty consists of the impossibility, before individual lengths of life are known, to identify the persons who will have a short life. A policy of compensation by anticipation would require to be able to identify—when they are still alive—the persons who will turn out to die prematurely in the future, and to give them, in an anticipatory form, some compensation for the harms that they will suffer in the future (due to their future premature death). However, such an anticipatory compensation policy is not possible, since no person can know the duration of life of persons as long as these persons are still alive. The only persons whose length of life is known consist of persons who are already deceased. For the other persons, there exists uncertainty about the duration of their life. Note that the existence of life expectancy statistics does not have any relevancy for the issue at stake, since the relevant informational basis for compensation by anticipation lies at the level of each individual. Since life expectancy statistics provide estimates of average lifetime at the level of a group of persons, these statistics can hardly help for the design of compensation policies by anticipation. The pieces of information required by anticipatory compensation policies are just not available: there remains a fundamental uncertainty about the length of each human life.

But these difficulties do not imply that there is an impossibility to construct a social insurance against a short life. Actually, this social insurance can be constructed, provided one rethinks the structure of the welfare state, as well as the allocation of resources along the human life cycle. The double impossibility highlighted above—the impossibility of ex post compensation and the impossibility of ex ante identification—does not completely close the door for the compensation, ex ante, of the harm caused by premature death.

[28] Life-insurances sold on the market are advantageous to the survivors of the deceased and benefit only indirectly to the deceased (in case of altruism towards the surviving siblings). But the problem with these private life-insurances is that these are quite expensive and can only benefit to persons who are sufficiently wealthy and benefit from some social network (family or friends), so that the payment of the premium to the survivors can improve the situation of the dead. We are thus far away from the social insurance against a short life that is studied in this book.

A key point to be noticed is that even though the persons who will turn out to die prematurely in the future cannot be identified when they are still alive (second impossibility) and cannot be compensated once the harm has occurred (first impossibility), it is nonetheless possible to improve the situation of these persons *when they are still alive.*

In order to compensate the persons who will die prematurely in the future despite the impossibility to identify these, it is sufficient to improve the quality of living conditions at the young age when all persons—including the ones who will die prematurely in the future—are still alive. Indeed, by increasing the well-being level of all individuals at the young ages, one must necessarily also improve the situation of the persons who will die prematurely. A social insurance against a short life is thus possible, provided one understands that the set of young persons includes the subset of persons who will die prematurely and have a short life. The fact that this subset cannot be precisely identified is not problematic and does not prevent the compensation of the harm suffered by the persons who will die prematurely. By improving the living conditions of all young persons, one improves also the situation of the non-identified subset of young persons who will turn out to have a short life.[29]

3.6 Herod's Strategy

A social insurance against a short life relies on two components. First, a statistical discrimination strategy that consists, in order to treat a non-identified group of persons, of extending the treatment to the smallest set of persons including necessarily, on the basis of the available information, the entire set of persons to be treated.[30] Second, a chronological age criterion allowing for the construction of the smallest set of persons

[29] Note that the possibility of an insurance against a short life does not necessary imply that this insurance is complete, and thus allows for the perfect equalization of the well-being levels of short-lived and long-lived persons. While such equalization is, in general, possible in a first-best world (i.e., with all policy instruments) under (some) substitutability between the quantity and the quality of life, it is generally not possible under more realistic conditions. On the conditions of completeness of compensation, see Fleurbaey et al. (2014).

[30] In the case of an insurance against a short life, the persons to be treated are these who will die prematurely in the future. The treatment in question consists of improving the situation of these persons, in order to neutralize the harm caused by a short life.

including, again on the basis of the available information, all persons to be treated.

In order to illustrate the first component of a social insurance against a short life—the treatment of a non-identified group by extension of the treatment to the smallest set of persons which includes all persons to be treated—let us refer to the Bible and more precisely to the writings of Saint Matthew. Saint Matthew describes a tragic episode of the Bible—the Massacre of the Innocents—that can help us understanding the logics at work behind a social insurance against a short life: treating a large number of persons to be sure to achieve the treatment of an unidentified subset of the population. Here is the relevant quote from the Bible (Matthews, Chapter 2, 13–18):

> 13 When they had gone, an angel of the Lord appeared to Joseph in a dream. "Get up," he said, "take the child and his mother and escape to Egypt. Stay there until I tell you, for Herod is going to search for the child to kill him."
> 14 So he got up, took the child and his mother during the night and left for Egypt, 15 where he stayed until the death of Herod. And so was fulfilled what the Lord had said through the prophet: "Out of Egypt I called my son."
> 16 When Herod realized that he had been outwitted by the Magi, he was furious, and he gave orders to kill all the boys in Bethlehem and its vicinity who were two years old and under, in accordance with the time he had learned from the Magi.

Herod, the king of Judea, does not know who the Messiah is, where he is born, where he lives. However, Herod has a significant piece of information: the Messiah is a baby. In order to reach his goal—the death of the Messiah—Herod ordered that all children aged less than 2 years are killed. That strategy consists of extending the treatment that he wants to impose to the Messiah (death) to the smallest set of persons who necessarily includes, on the basis of the available pieces of information, the person to be treated. Since Herod knew the age of the child (less than 2 years), and no other piece of information, he constructed the smallest set of persons including the person to be treated (the Messiah) by using an age criterion.

The construction of a social insurance against the risk of a short life shares some structural characteristics with the problem faced by the King Herod. There is a non-identified set of persons that should be treated:

these are the persons who will have a premature death, the ones that an insurance against a short life aims at compensating. In order to achieve that goal, a possible strategy is to follow Herod's strategy: *in order to treat a set of non-identified persons, one has to extend the treatment to the smallest set of persons that necessarily includes, on the basis of the available information, the persons to be treated.*

How can one justify the relevancy of Herod's strategy for the design of an insurance against a short life? Each form of statistical discrimination solves, in a context of imperfect information, a trade-off between reducing the number of type I errors (i.e., treating persons that should not be treated) and reducing the number of type II errors (i.e., not treating persons that should be treated).[31] Herod's strategy aims at minimizing the number of type II errors and thus gives priority to the goal of compensating the full set of persons who will turn out to die prematurely in the future, even at the cost of treating also some persons who will not die prematurely.[32]

Having justified the relevancy of Herod's strategy for the design of an insurance against a short life, we still have to justify the second component of that insurance device: the reliance on a criterion based on the chronological age in order to define the set of persons including all persons to be treated. At first glance, many other criteria could be used to construct that set of persons and to determine the population to be treated. Why should we rely on the chronological age?

We believe that, in the current state of knowledge, the most relevant criterion to define the set of persons to be treated for the design of an insurance against a short life consists of the belonging to an age group, that is, a group whose members have an age inferior to a threshold defined in terms of chronological age. The reliance on a criterion defined in terms of chronological age is justified by the fact that relying on other criteria would not allow to treating all persons that should be treated, because of the multiplicity of the causes of death. In other words, relying on other

[31] In the case of criminal justice, type I errors consist of condemning innocent persons, whereas type II errors consist of not condemning guilty persons.

[32] Minimizing the number of type II errors could, at first glance, seem inadequate, because criminal justice, which guarantees that the doubt benefits to the accused person, gives priority to the minimization of the number of type I errors. But it should be reminded that criminal justice distributes penalties, whereas the design of a social insurance against a short life is about distributing compensations. For that particular task, it is plausible to give priority to the minimization of the number of type II errors.

criteria would lead to define a set of persons that would not include all persons who will, in the future, have a short life.

Let us suppose, for instance, that researchers can identify the 'longevity gene', i.e., a genetic characteristic that is associated with a long life. One could then expect that the compensation of the persons who will die prematurely could be achieved by first testing all individuals in the population and, then, by supplying compensations to individuals whose genetic background does not include the 'longevity gene'. But the problem is that the set of persons who do not have the 'longevity gene' does not include all the persons who will have a short life. Due to the multiplicity of the causes of death (accidents, etc.), some individuals who do have the 'longevity gene' in their genetic background will nonetheless die prematurely. A genetic criterion cannot allow to constructing the subset of the population that includes *all* persons who will turn out to die prematurely.[33]

In the current state of scientific knowledge, the best candidate for the construction of a set including all persons who will have a short life consists of a criterion based on the chronological age. Actually, all persons who will die prematurely in the future have been alive at some moment and thus have belonged to some young age groups. Thus, targeting the set of persons whose chronological age lies below some threshold allows us to treat the persons who will have a premature death.

In sum, the obstacle of non-identification of the persons who will die prematurely can be overcome by adopting a particular form of statistical discrimination—Herod's strategy—combined with a criterion based on chronological age. Exactly as Herod could not identify the Messiah within the population, the welfare state cannot identify the persons who will turn out to die prematurely in the future. Moreover, in the same way as Herod overcomes the non-identification of the Messiah by targeting all children of the same age as the Messiah, the welfare state can overcome the non-identification of the future short-lived persons by improving the situation of all young adults. Only a divine intervention made Herod's strategy fail. But in the absence of any divine intervention, an insurance against a short life relying on the logic of Herod's strategy will not fail. An insurance against a short life is thus possible, despite the difficulties

[33] Because of the same reason, a criterion based on the biological age (degree of deterioration of organs) could not include all persons who will have a short life.

underlined above. A solution to the problem exists and takes the form of a simple maxim, which we will now examine.

3.7 A Maxim for the Allocation of Resources

Adopting the logic of Herod's strategy, the design of a social insurance against the risk of a short life can rely on a maxim stating that resources should be allocated in such a way as to improve the situation of all young individuals[34]:

> *In order to set up a social insurance against the risk of a short life, the welfare state should concentrate the good things of life at young ages, and postpone the less good things of life to higher ages.*

This maxim invites two remarks. First, the maxim does not concern the allocation of all resources, but, only, the allocation of some resources, which are considered either as *universally* good or as *universally* bad, what we call the 'good things of life' and the 'less good things of life'. This restriction comes from a double imperfection of the informational environment. On the one hand, the persons who will turn out to die prematurely are not identifiable when they are still alive, as we have seen previously. On the other hand, there exists a multitude of conceptions of the good life, so that one cannot identify what matters for the persons who will turn out to die prematurely in the future. This double informational imperfection implies that a compensation device based on Herod's strategy must, to be efficient, rely on the allocation of resources regarded as universally good or universally bad, whatever the age or the preferences of individuals are.

A second point should be underlined: applying the above maxim of resource allocation allows to reducing the harm caused by a premature death through two distinct channels. First, by allocating the good things of life at young ages, the welfare state would make these good things available to all individuals, whatever these persons enjoy a long life or a short

[34] We consider here the challenges raised by the construction of a social insurance against a short life, by means of the design of a new pillar of the welfare state. We will consider self-insurance strategies later on, but only in a secondary way, because cognitive obstacles make such self-insurance strategies inefficient, thus inviting a corrective intervention by the welfare state (see infra).

life. This will improve the situation of the persons who will die prematurely. Second, by concentrating the less good things of life to higher ages, the maxim makes these unpleasant things inaccessible to the persons who will die prematurely. This improves the situation of the persons who will have a short life. But a corollary of this is the deterioration of the life-years lived at older ages. The additional life-years that would have been lived in the absence of a premature death are thus of less good quality, which reduces welfare losses due to a short life.

The setting under study plays the role of an insurance device against a short life, in the precise sense that applying the maxim contributes to reduce the harm caused by the event of a premature death. The application of that maxim for the allocation of resources guarantees a compensation for the victims of an early death: this mechanism improves the situation of the persons who have a short life (i.e., in economic terms, makes these persons better off), while reducing the harm caused by a short life. In other words, this device transfers resources from good states of nature (a long life) to bad states of nature (a short life), in line with basic insurance principles. This compensation takes place despite the impossibility to identify—when they are still alive—the persons who will die prematurely.

However, it should be stressed that this maxim of allocation of resources, as it is currently stated, may lead to a somewhat paradoxical situation. By concentrating the 'good things' of life at the beginning of life and the 'bad things' at higher ages, it could be possible—at least in theory—to make a short life *better* than a long life. When applied in that manner, the maxim would no longer be compatible with the ideal of compensation that governed its foundation. In order to avoid this, it is useful to rewrite the maxim as follows:

> *In order to set up a social insurance against the risk of a short life, the welfare state should concentrate the good things of life at young ages, and postpone the less good things of life to higher ages, and do so until the well-being level associated with a short life is as close as possible to the well-being level associated with a long life.*

This reformulation of the maxim imposes a limit concerning the extent to which the good things of life should be concentrated at young ages and the bad things of life postponed to older ages. For sure, the pursued goal here is to insure individuals against the risk of having a short life and, thus, to improve the situation of the short-lived, but not to turn the luck of being long-lived into a calamity. The insurance against a short life should definitely not make long-lived individuals worse off than short-lived persons.

Importantly, adopting the above maxim for resource allocation has strong corollaries for the structure of the welfare state. If one considers that leisure time or free time is a 'good thing' of life, and if the working time is regarded as a 'less good' thing in life, the maxim provides nothing less than foundations for the construction of a reverse retirement system. Actually, under these hypotheses, a system of reverse retirement would concentrate a good thing of life—leisure time or free time—early in life, and a less good thing—work—for older ages, in line with the maxim for a just allocation of resources.[35]

But before considering this policy corollary in more details—Chapter 4 of this book is entirely dedicated to systems of reverse retirement—it is crucial, at this stage, to ask the question of the social desirability of a maxim of resource allocation requiring to concentrate the 'good things' of life early in life and the 'less good things' later on in life. Is it socially desirable to organize the allocation of resources in this manner?

The answer to this question depends on the underlying concept of social justice. If, for instance, one adopts a utilitarian point of view, the above maxim lacks foundations, because it leads to a lower social welfare—i.e., sum of individual utilities—in comparison with what would prevail if the resources were allocated in a more smooth way along the ages of life.[36] Alternatively, if one adopts a Rawlsian conception of social justice, the maxim can also be criticized. Indeed, Rawls was opposed to all forms of discriminations. But the problem is that the maxim recommends some form of age discrimination favouring the young.

But one should not exaggerate the scope of these criticisms. If one adopts the view of social justice as 'to each according to one's needs', the compensation of short-lived persons is a priority, and the maxim

[35] Note that the reallocation of working time towards older ages as required by the second formulation of the maxim should not make a long life worse than a short life. As a consequence, if one assumes that the disutility of labour is higher at old ages, this maxim justifies the existence of an age of (final) exit from work (see Chapter 4).

[36] It can be shown in a dynamic overlapping generation model that, under general conditions, a reverse retirement system is never socially optimal under utilitarianism. See Ponthiere (2020).

that we studied is justified as a means to achieve the compensation of the short-lived. True, the maxim justifies some form of age-based statistical discrimination, but such discrimination is the price to pay in order to bring compensation to the persons who die prematurely, and who have more urgent needs to live good things during their (short) life.[37] Criticizing the maxim on the grounds of its implications for *senior* persons—while minimizing its positive effects on the lives of the short-lived—does not do justice to the heavy and arbitrary harms suffered by the short-lived, which, as such, require compensation. Such a critique of the maxim is thus even more questionable than the maxim itself, if one is egalitarian and wants to defend social justice.

In sum, the maxim of resource allocation formulated in this chapter can serve for the design of a social insurance against the risk of a short life.[38] As such, this maxim can provide foundations for the construction of a new welfare state, which would be more just, by paying more attention to the satisfaction of the needs of the most disadvantaged persons: the unlucky persons who turn out to die prematurely.

Several obstacles exist and make the application of that maxim difficult. Our societies yield an allocation of resources that is often the *inverse* of the one required by the maxim. Standard retirement systems concentrate leisure time—a good thing—at old ages, whereas work—a less pleasant thing—is done during young adulthood. These gaps between, on the one hand, what the maxim recommends and, on the other hand, the functioning of our societies are not due to a lack of chance: these reveal the existence of cognitive biases leading to an allocation of working time that goes against what an insurance against a short life would require. Let us now discuss these biases, which are major obstacles preventing the emergence of a social insurance against a short life.

[37] We are here in a situation where a particular form of discrimination can make us closer to the ideal of social justice. On the relations between discriminations and social justice, see Lippert-Rasmussen (2018).

[38] Note that the proposed device is not, *stricto* sensu, an 'insurance' in the particular sense proposed by Arrow (1965, p. 45), that is, 'the exchange of money now for money payable contingent on the occurrence of certain events'. However, relying on Herod strategy allows to construct a device that constitutes an insurance device when one defines 'insurance' more broadly, as a 'means or a procedure that reduces uncertainty about the future' (Zweifel and Eisen 2012, p. 3). The present essay relies on the latter definition of 'insurance'.

3.8 The Denial of Death

The most important obstacle against the setting of an insurance against a short life consists of the denial of death. Denying the temporal finiteness of human beings is an old attitude. In *On the Shortness of Life*, Seneca criticized, about 2,000 years ago, men who are unable to acknowledge their status of simple mortal beings, and who live *as if* they will always live. They feel invulnerable and they wait until high ages to retire from business and to start looking for wisdom. 'What foolish forgetfulness of mortality to postpone wholesome plans to the fiftieth and sixtieth year, and to intend to begin life at a point to which few have attained!' Seneca further asked: 'And what guarantee, pray, have you that your life will last longer? Who will suffer your course to be just as you plan it?'.[39]

But if humans have difficulties to acknowledge the finiteness of their existence, how could they support an insurance against a short life? If the possibility of an early death is left aside, why should one insure oneself against such an event?

The non-insurance against nasty events regarded as unlikely constitutes a general problem for insurance economics. As underlined by Daniel Kahneman, individuals have a tendency to underestimate the probabilities of occurrence of negative events, because of an excessive optimism.[40] This optimistic bias reduces the demand for private insurance contracts. An illustration of this problem for insurance markets lies in the case of insurance against risks of long-term care. Elderly individuals face high risks of loss of autonomy, leading to large long-term care expenditures (including nursing homes or home care). The objective probability of falling one day in old-age dependency is about 50% for women and 33% for men. But when one asks individuals about their perceived magnitudes of these risks, subjective probabilities are much lower than objective probabilities: about 50% of the surveyed persons believe that they face a zero probability to fall into old-age dependency in the future.[41] In the light of these low subjective probabilities, it is no surprise that only a small minority of the population does purchase private long-term care insurance.[42]

[39] See Seneca, *On the Shortness of Life*, III.

[40] See Kahneman (2011).

[41] See Finkelstein and McGarry (2006).

[42] Note that this bias is only one explanation—among others—of the low demand for private long-term care insurance. On this, see Pestieau and Ponthiere (2012).

The bias towards optimism makes persons underestimate the probability of occurrence of harms in the future, and, hence, it leads them not to purchase private insurance contracts against the occurrence of these harms, even if possible harms are substantial. One can reasonably think that these cognitive biases are general, and concern a large class of risks, including the risk of a premature death.

In this early twenty-first century, death is a kind of unthought of our societies. But this has not always been the case. As Ariès underlined in *Western Attitudes Toward Death*, men and women have, during the longest part of history, been quite familiar with death, which was lived as a collective event. The strength of mortality having remained high (at a rate of about 1 out of 30) across centuries, humans have been continuously facing death. Each death was prepared in advance, and the death of a person was accompanied by rituals accomplished within ceremonies (before the death and after the death): this was the epoch of what Ariès called the 'tamed death' (*mort apprivoisée*)[43]:

> People had been dying like that for centuries or millennia. In a world of change the traditional attitude toward death appears inert and static. The old attitude in which death was both familiar and near, evoking no great fear or awe, offers too marked a contrast to ours, where death is so frightful that we dare not utter its name. This is why I have called this household sort of death "tamed death". I do not mean that death had once been wild and that it had ceased to be so. I mean, on the contrary, that today it has become wild.

The status of death has changed across centuries. According to Ariès, three steps have followed the era of the 'tamed death'. During the twelfth century, death stopped being a collectively lived phenomenon and became individualized. The individualization of death is illustrated by Ariès by means of the evolution, over time, of the representation of the Judgement Day. Initially, the Judgement Day was a collective event, concerning humanity as a whole, at the end of all times. But progressively, the Judgement Day has changed in nature, to become a judgement concerning a single person, at the end of her life, as a kind of 'life check-up'. Then, starting in the eighteenth century, death has become more emotional and passionate. Under the influence of the coming romantic period, death

[43] See Ariès (1974, pp. 13–14).

was no longer lived as a common natural phenomenon, falling under the laws of Nature, but as a dramatic break up: this is the age of the romantic death, the age of 'the death of the other'. Finally, in the twentieth century, medical progress has deeply changed the status of death. The death is no longer lived collectively around rituals within the community of the future deceased. On the contrary, individuals die alone in hospital rooms, almost in secret. According to Ariès, death has become, in the twentieth century, a kind of forbidden, a kind of taboo, because it goes against the dominant imperative of happiness[44]:

> But the interdict on death suddenly follows upon the heels of a very long period – several centuries – in which death was a public spectacle from which no one would have thought of hiding and which was ever sought after at times. The cause of the interdict is at once apparent: the need for happiness – the moral duty and the social obligation to contribute to the collective happiness by avoiding any cause for sadness or boredom, by appearing to be always happy, even if in the depths of despair. By showing the least sign of sadness, one sins against happiness, threatens it, and society then risks losing its *raison d'être*.

According to Ariès, the most common attitude towards death is, in the twentieth century, a kind of forbidden of death, aimed at preserving the ideal of collective happiness. Medical progress in men's struggle against death has made death less familiar and has transformed it into a kind of taboo. In the capitalist society, where everyone has to be productive, healthy and smiling, death has become what Ariès calls the 'unspeakable'.

Death being a kind of taboo, the question of the insurance against a premature death can hardly be asked. If men and women do not want to think about dying in the future, why would they demand an insurance against the risk of an early death? In a world where death is not nameable any longer—and thus can hardly be discussed—an insurance against a premature death looks useless or even irrelevant.

But how is it possible to live *as if* the risk of death were absent? This question lies at the very heart of the essay *La Mort* (*Death*) by Vladimir Jankelevitch. According to Jankelevitch, death is seen as a universal law, which concerns all living beings. But at the level of individual psychology, this universal law does not tell anything about the particular event that is

[44] See Ariès (1974, pp. 93–94).

personal death. A person does not regard herself as one case among many others. A person considers that her life is a special case, precisely because it is *her* own life. Persons do 'as if' death concerned only the others—but not themselves. Then, due to the strength of habits, they end up forgetting about their reliance on the 'as if' proviso.

This tendency to exclude oneself from what is regarded as a universal law is reinforced by the fact that, although death is certain (*mors certa*), the time or date of death is uncertain (*hora incerta*). This uncertainty about the age at death can make the individual believe that it is 'as if' the event of his death had become (also) uncertain. According to Jankelevitch, the uncertainty about the future moment of death creates a 'maybe': maybe death will not concern me? This 'maybe' can generate a hope of immortality[45]:

> Fear, trembling and suspicion whispered: the time is uncertain, but as the fact is certain, be prepared for any eventuality. And now the confident and reassured man says to himself: The time is uncertain? All in good time! All hopes are therefore permitted. [...] The certainty of dying, shaken by indeterminacy and the contingent nature of the date, is no longer, after all, so certain! This is how the contingency of the hour goes up to our heads, so to speak, and finally casts doubt on the most certain thing in the world: as it is never necessary to die of such and such a disease, nor to such or such date, the man, drunk with senseless hopes, begins to wonder if it is so necessary to die in general.

The denial of death makes the insurance against a short life useless. Someone who does as if death will not concern oneself cannot find any interest in being insured against a premature death. However, this attitude is senseless: death is inevitable, and the risks of a premature death exist, and do not only concern the others.

As for other insurance devices, the irrationality of men and women makes them underestimate the risk of being harmed and, also, the size of the harm. These cognitive biases imply that individuals, if left alone when facing these choices, would probably purchase no or only little insurance. This kind of irrationality invites, as a remedy, some form of public intervention. Indeed, this is one of the major functions of the welfare

[45] See Jankelevitch (1977, p. 149) (translated by the author).

state: correcting individual biases and the consequences of lack of rationality. For that purpose, the welfare state can build insurance devices that allow to protect citizens against their irrationality and, also, against their senseless hopes.

What is true for the insurance against lots of risks is also true for the insurance against the risk of dying prematurely. If the mechanisms studied by Ariès and Jankelevitch are at work, a person considers death as something that does not concern her or may concern her only in a distant future. As a consequence, there is little chance that she purchases insurance protecting her against a premature death, even though harms caused by an early death are substantial. Thus, the denial of death provides a reason to include the insurance against a short life within the set of mandatory insurance devices supplied by the welfare state. When facing the person's denial of death, the welfare state should supply an insurance device, in order to protect citizens against the risk of a premature death. Protecting citizens against the risk of a short life amounts also to protecting them against senseless hopes of immortality.

3.9 The Bias Towards the Future

The denial of death is not the sole obstacle preventing the setting of an insurance against a short life. A second obstacle consists of the attitudes of humans when facing different times of their life, and, in particular, when facing their future. In *On the Shortness of Life*, Seneca criticized humans' tendency to waste their lifetime, by remaining suspended to the future. The exaggerated weight assigned to the future prevented humans from living their life fully.

Closer to us, Derek Parfit analysed the tendency of being suspended to the future. As we have seen when studying the Surgery Case, Parfit's patient prefers the certainty of a long and painful surgery in the past over the certainty of short surgery in the future. Parfit considers that this bias towards the future constitutes a harmful trait of human psychology. According to Parfit, humans would benefit from becoming *timeless* individuals, who treat all their life-periods in a similar way, without assigning too much weight to the future.

This bias towards the future constitutes a major obstacle against the construction of an insurance against the short life. Remind that such insurance would be based on a simple maxim: concentrate, to some extent, the 'good things of life' in young ages and the 'bad things of life' at older ages. Applying this maxim would make all young adults better off and, hence, would also improve the situation of the unlucky persons who will die prematurely. But that compensation of the short-lived has also a cost: the worsening of life at senior ages.

By implying, for each life, a more gloomy future, the insurance against a short life could attract lots of criticisms. If humans exhibit what Parfit called a bias towards the future, they will have a tendency to value strongly, in their life, not what they have already lived, but *what remains to be lived*. But this is precisely what the application of the maxim tends to deteriorate: by allocating the 'good things of life' at the beginning of life, one must necessarily make the remaining of life less attractive. Thus, persons valuing strongly their future are likely to be unenthusiastic for the construction of an insurance against a short life.

But the existence of a bias towards the future does not imply that one should give up the construction of an insurance against the risk of a premature death. Actually, the existence of these cognitive biases underlines only that a *decentralized* system of insurance against a short life cannot emerge spontaneously. The attitude of persons with respect to their future is such that it is highly unlikely that they demand for an insurance against the risk of a short life. As a consequence of this low demand, it is also unlikely that insurance companies decide to supply such insurance. At the end of the day, the market supplies no insurance against a short life, and individuals suffering from a bias towards the future will not either insure themselves by their own strategies (self-insurance).

It is precisely for these reasons that it is necessary that the welfare state organizes a device allowing citizens to be insured against the risk of a short life: spontaneously, persons will not choose to organize such insurance. Constructing an insurance against a short life requires thus a coordinating intervention at a higher level, the one of the welfare states.

3.10 Towards a New Pillar for the Welfare State

Since its construction in the middle of the twentieth century, the modern welfare state insures citizens against various risks of life: the risk of disease (health insurance), the risk of job loss (unemployment insurance) and the risk of a family (family allowances), among other risks. In order to offer a universal social security, the welfare state acts as the major insurer of our lives: it organizes the (mandatory) payment of contributions to various public funds, and, in case of harm, it provides compensatory allocations to the victims.[46]

Why do these insurance devices rely on the coercive action of the state, rather than on private insurance markets? Various factors explain this. On the demand side, individuals have a tendency, as we have seen, to underestimate the probability of occurrence of events leading to harms, which reduces spontaneous demand for insurance. This leads to the necessity, for the welfare state, to impose some form of mandatory insurance, which corrects for individual myopia and cognitive biases. Of course, such a compulsory insurance could still be supplied by private firms, but then a large number of persons being in poverty would not be covered. On the supply side, the insurance market suffers from serious imperfections: imperfect competition due to scale effects and asymmetries of information leading to the attrition of the market. Because of all these reasons, the state plays a strong role in the insurance domain.

But if the welfare state insures citizens against disease, unemployment and the family, why does it not insure them against the risk of a short life?

In our view, there exist good reasons why such insurance should be constructed: this would bring back some justice in a world where individuals have unequal longevity. Premature deaths impose heavy harms to the unlucky short-lived. An insurance against a short life would distribute the burden of this harm on a larger number of persons, in such a way as to avoid the concentration of the whole burden on a few shoulders. *Sharing—rather than concentrating—the losses: the insurance against a short life would be a major step towards more social justice.* The next chapter will demonstrate that a reverse retirement system can constitute the cornerstone of an insurance against a short life.

References

Ariès, Philippe. 1974. *Western Attitudes Toward Death*. Baltimore: Johns Hopkins University Press.

Arrow, Kenneth. 1965. *Aspects of the Theory of Risk-Bearing*. Helsinki: Yrjo Johnsson Lectures.

Balia, Silvia, and Andrew Jones. 2008. 'Mortality, Lifestyles and Socioeconomic Status'. *Journal of Health Economics* 27: 1–26.

[46] See Laroque (1948).

Barr, Nicholas, and Peter Diamond. 2003. 'The Economics of Pensions'. *Oxford Review of Economic Policy* 22: 15–39.
Barr, Nicholas, and Peter Diamond. 2008. *Reforming Pensions*. Oxford: Oxford University Press.
Bentham, Jeremy. 1789. *An Introdution to the Principles of Morals and Legislation*. Oxford: Clarendon Press.
Bommier, Antoine, Thierry Magnac, Benoît Rapoport, and Muriel Roger. 2006. 'Droits à la retraite et mortalité différentielle'. *Economie Et Prévisions* 168: 1–16.
Christensen, Kaare, Thomas Johnson, and James Vaupel. 2006. 'The Quest for Genetic Determinants of Human Longevity: Challenges and Insights'. *Nature Genetics* 7: 436–448.
Coronado, Julia Lynn, Don Fullerton, and Thomas Glass. 2011. 'The Progressivity of Social Security'. *The B.E. Journal of Economic Analysis and Policy* 11: 1–45.
Cremer, Helmuth, and Pierre Pestieau. 2011. 'Myopia, Redistribution and Pensions'. *European Economic Review* 55: 165–175.
Finkelstein, Amy, and Katherine McGarry. 2006. 'Multiple Dimensions of Private Information: Evidence from the Long-Term Care Insurance Market'. *American Economic Review* 96: 938–958.
Fleurbaey, Marc. 2009. *Fairness, Responsibility and Welfare*. Oxford: Oxford University Press.
Fleurbaey, Marc, Marie-Louise Leroux, and Gregory Ponthiere. 2014. 'Compensating the Dead'. *Journal of Mathematical Economics* 51: 28–41.
Jankelevitch, Vladimir. 1977. *La mort*. Paris: Flammarion.
Jevons, William Stanley. 1871. *The Theory of Political Economy*. London: Pellican Books.
Kahneman, Daniel. 2011. *Thinking, Fast and Slow*. London: Allen Lane.
Laroque, Pierre. 1948. 'De l'assurance sociale à la sécurité sociale: l'expérience sociale'. *Revue Internationale du Travail* LVII : 621–649
Lippert-Rasmussen, Kasper. 2018. 'Discriminations'. *Oxford Handbook of Distributive Justice*. Oxford: Oxford University Press.
Marx, Karl. 1875. *Critique of the Gotha Program*. New York: International Publishers.
Miller, David. 1976. *Social Justice*. Oxford: Oxford University Press.
Mirrlees, James. 1982. 'The Economic Uses of Utilitarianism'. In *Utilitarianism and Beyond*, edited by A.K. Sen and B. Williams. Cambridge: Cambridge University Press.
Moore, G.E. 1912. *Principia Ethica*. Cambridge: Cambridge University Press.
Pestieau, Pierre, and Gregory Ponthiere. 2012. 'Long Term Care Insurance Puzzle'. In *Financing Long-Term Care in Europe: Institutions, Markets and*

Models, edited by J. Costa-Font, and C. Courbage. Basingstoke: Palgrave Macmillan.

Ponthiere, Gregory. 2020. 'A Theory of Reverse Retirement'. *Journal of Public Economic Theory* 22: 1618–1659.

Rawls, John. 1971. *A Theory of Justice*. Cambridge: Harvard University Press.

Sen, Amartya. 1980. 'Equality of What?' *Tanner Lectures on Human Values*. Utah: University of Utah Press.

Zweifel, Peter, and Roland Eisen. 2012. *Insurance Economics*. Heidelberg: Springer.

CHAPTER 4

Reversing Retirement Systems

Abstract Age-based statistical discrimination favouring the young would lead us to a major reform of existing pension systems. Transferring 'good things of life', such as consumption and free time, to young ages, and 'less good things of life', such as labour, to older ages, implies that existing pension systems should be partly reversed: instead of having a unique retirement period at the end of the life cycle, one should offer also a period of retirement to all young adults before they start their career. Young adults would, during that initial retirement period, earn a pension allowance, which would be financed by postponing the age of final retirement for senior workers. This partial 'reversal' of pension systems would thus contribute to insure all citizens against the risk of a short life, because the retirement period would then be enjoyed by all persons at the beginning of adulthood, including the persons who will die prematurely. This chapter examines the demographic and technical conditions under which such a partial reversal of pension systems is possible. It is argued that the current age structure of the population in advanced economies, as well as the current technical conditions making labour less physically-demanding, are more favourable than ever before from the perspective of reversing pension systems. This Chapter examines the design of key parameters of the reform as well as various criticisms against this reform of pension systems.

G. Ponthiere, *Allocating Pensions to Younger People*,
https://doi.org/10.1007/978-3-031-24748-4_4

Keywords Pension systems · Retirement age · Age-based statistical discrimination · Reverse retirement · Age structure

Concentrating the 'good things of life' at young ages, and postponing the 'bad things of life' to older ages. This is the maxim whose reasonable application would reduce the harm caused by a short life, and, hence, would serve the ideal of insurance against premature death. Applying this maxim would also decrease the scope of injustice due to longevity inequalities.

Is it possible to apply that maxim of resource allocation to real-world economies? By what means could one reallocate or transfer the 'good things of life' to young ages, and the 'less good things' to older ages?

This chapter argues that the construction of a reverse retirement system could allow for an application of this maxim in real-world economies. A system of reverse retirement could bring our societies closer to the ideal of social justice, despite longevity inequalities.[1] By a 'system of reverse retirement', I mean a retirement system where senior workers would finance pension allowances paid to young adults, unlike in existing pension systems.[2] In a reverse retirement system, young adults would benefit of a retirement period *before* starting their career. *Whereas existing retirement systems require that individuals work during several decades before having the right to retire, a reverse retirement system would allow young adults to enjoy a retirement period before they start working.*

A system of reverse retirement would exhibit two important characteristics.

On the one hand, the reverse retirement system would not be optional, but would be *mandatory*, like the other pillars of the welfare state, such

[1] In the Appendix, we compare the reverse retirement system with other potential insurance devices against the risk of a short life (such as standard life insurance contracts or inheritance taxation differentiated on the basis of the age of the deceased). We show that these other devices exhibit a lower coverage of the population at risk in comparison to reverse retirement.

[2] This kind of reverse retirement system would be of the pay-as-you-go type, in the sense that pension allowances paid to young adults during a year would be financed by contributions paid by workers during the same year. The difference with respect to existing pay-as-you-go pension systems would concern the definition of the ages of contributors and beneficiaries of the pension system (see infra).

as the unemployment insurance and the health insurance. The mandatory nature of the reverse retirement system can be justified as follows. If the possibility to enjoy an initial period of retirement before starting the career were left to the free choice of individuals, the denial of death and the bias towards the future could, as we have seen in Chapter 3, encourage persons to give up the reverse retirement device. This attitude would prevent the realization of a social insurance against the risk of a short life.[3]

On the other hand, the reversal of pension systems that we will study in this chapter consists of a *partial* reversal of existing pension systems. In that new system, pension allowances given to young adults would be financed by the work of senior workers, but there would still exist an age beyond which senior persons would enjoy a retirement period, and would irreversibly leave the labour market. As a consequence, a system of reverse retirement would divide the adult life cycle in three stages: an initial retirement period, then a working period (the career), and, finally, a second, final retirement period. The latter is justified by the low productivity of very old workers and by the very high disutility of labour at high ages. Thus we find here the classical function of a retirement period: guaranteeing a decent life to the persons who are too old to be able to work.[4]

Could such a reversal of pension systems reallocate the 'good things of life' at young ages? Could reverse retirement contribute to insure citizens against the risk of a short life?

The basic postulates of economic analysis tell us that the consumption of goods and services, as well as the enjoyment of leisure time, are desirable goods, i.e., goods that one prefers to have in a larger quantity rather than in a smaller quantity. On the contrary, since Jevons's pioneer work *The Theory of Political Economy*, working time is modelled as a source of disutility, that is, as an undesirable good. Under these classical hypotheses,

[3] See the Appendix on a more detailed justification of the mandatory nature of the junior work ban involved in a reverse retirement system.

[4] When retirement systems were generalized after 1945 across Europe, the age of 60 years was a good proxy of the critical age threshold beyond which labour productivity is too low and labour disutility is too high to work. But nowadays, at the age of 60 years, workers have still strong physical and mental capacities, which allow them to keep on contributing to the productive effort of the society. The age threshold has thus moved, and reverse retirement systems should take this new age threshold into account.

the reverse retirement system reallocates 'good things of life' (consumption and leisure) at young ages, and 'bad things of life' (working time) at higher ages, in line with the maxim of Chapter 3.[5]

At first glance, this rationale looks solid and well-founded. However, as we shall see, it is *only under some conditions* that a system of reverse retirement can actually satisfy the maxim describing a just allocation of resources. In some cases, reversing pension systems could, at the end of the day, deteriorate living standards at the young age, and, hence, could worsen the situation of the unlucky short-lived, in opposition to what an insurance against a short life recommends. This counterintuitive result is due to the fact that the available resources in an economy do not exist in a fixed quantity, but depend on how working time is allocated across the different ages of life. Reallocating working time towards senior ages could, under some conditions, impoverish the economy and make the young worse-off. In such circumstances, the reverse retirement system would not contribute to improve the situation of the short-lived, and, hence, would not serve the ideal of an insurance against a premature death.

When considering issues of social architecture, the devil is in the details. This chapter aims at examining the conditions under which the reversal of retirement systems could really serve the construction of a social insurance against the risk of a short life.

4.1 A Unique Opportunity in History

In *On the Shortness of Life*, Seneca blamed the men who wait until reaching age 50 or 60 to start living their life. But could it be feasible, at the time of Seneca, to set up a reverse retirement system? Could one, in the first century AC, repair the harms due to a premature death by allowing young adults to enjoy an initial period of retirement financed by the work of senior persons?

Unambiguously, the answer is: No. If, at the time of Seneca, one had constructed a reverse retirement system, that policy reform would not have contributed to improve living standards of young adults (and, hence,

[5] One could object to this that working is a necessary condition for individual flourishing and for social integration. When this is indeed the case, young individuals could work benevolently during their initial retirement period. As we shall see, a reverse retirement system would allow young adults to work benevolently (for instance in NGOs).

of the short-lived), but, rather, would have made them worse-off. Actually, in the first century of our era, the demography was characterized by a high mortality and by a high fertility.[6] Life expectancy at birth was 25 years. The pyramid of ages had a very wide basis, and an extremely narrow summit, because very few people could reach high ages. Thus populations were, at that time, composed mainly of children and young adults, whereas senior people were (in relative terms) not numerous.

Given the form of the age structure prevailing in the Antiquity, a system of reverse retirement would not have served the interests of short-lived persons. The reason is the following. The low proportion of seniors in the population at that time—in comparison to the large groups of young adults—would have implied a very low level of production per capita. This low output per capita would have led to massive poverty. Due to the imbalance between the number of beneficiaries (the number of young adults) and the number of contributors (the number of seniors), a system of reverse retirement would only have been able to give very low pension allowances to the young adults, thus making the life of the short-lived hardly valuable.

Besides the shape of the age structure, another factor would have also limited the level of pension allowances paid to young adults under a reverse retirement system. At the time of Seneca, production techniques were highly labour-intensive: human labour constituted, with land, the major input in the production process.[7] Works in the fields and in the workshops were highly physical, and required physical power and vigour. Thus, it made lots of sense to reserve working tasks for the young, who had the strongest working capacity, as well as the best physical reliance. Given the very low productivity of seniors in highly physical tasks, an economy relying on the labour of the old would have been characterized by a very low level of production, and by an extreme scarcity of resources.

Few senior workers (in relative terms) with a low productivity: as a consequence, the construction of a reverse retirement system would, at the time of Seneca, have caused mass poverty. Everyone would have then suffered from low living standards, including young adults, and, hence, including also the persons who have a short life. Thus, reverse retirement would have failed providing a social insurance against premature

[6] See Lee (2003).

[7] On the evolution of production techniques over the long period, see North (1981).

death. Note that this diagnosis applies not only to societies in the Antiquity, but, also, to most societies that existed along human history. During the longest part of history, a system of reverse retirement would not have been socially desirable, because high mortality would have implied a too low ratio of contributors over beneficiaries, leading to extremely low living standards and pensions, and, also, because the labour productivity of senior workers would have been too low to allow for the survival of the society under a reverse retirement system.

But let us come back in the twenty-first century. In our modern societies, could a reverse retirement system serve as a social insurance against the risk of a short life, and, hence, make our societies closer to the ideal of social justice?

The answer goes as follows. Our modern economies differ from the one at the time of Seneca on many fundamental aspects. These structural differences leave the *possibility* of a reverse retirement system open.[8]

A first thing to notice is that survival conditions are, nowadays, far more favourable than during the Antiquity. Life expectancy at birth is no longer as low as 25 years, but is now above 80 years in most advanced economies. This low mortality has important demographic corollaries concerning the shape of the age structure: a large proportion of the population reaches high ages of life. The proportion of seniors (in comparison to young adults) is now much larger than at the time of Seneca. Hence, the age structure prevailing in modern societies is much more balanced across age groups, and, hence, much more favourable for the purpose of constructing a reverse retirement system. The imbalance between the number of beneficiaries (young adults and the very old adults) and the number of contributors (senior adults) within this system is now less sizeable than it used to be.

But other key dimensions of our societies have evolved over time. Being aged 65 in the twenty-first century is not the same as being aged 65 at the time of Seneca. The chronological age—that is, the age determined by the date of birth—is no longer mechanically linked to the biological age—that is, the overall health status of the person—as it used to

[8] Ponthiere (2020a) derives the formal conditions on structural parameters of the economy (concerning demography, production and preferences) under which a reverse retirement system maximizes the realized well-being of the short-lived in a 4-period dynamic overlapping generations model.

be during the longest part of history.[9] Senior persons enjoy nowadays a better health in comparison to the health enjoyed by the old several centuries ago. For sure, senior persons can now contribute more than ever before to the production of goods and services. As a consequence, a modern economy based on the labour of senior workers would not fall into mass poverty.

Moreover, with the passage of time, production techniques have evolved: tools and machines—nowadays computers and automata—tend to make man's labour less demanding from a purely physical perspective. Requirements in terms of physical strength and body resilience are not the same as under previous production techniques. Working being less painful than before, the possibility of a larger involvement of senior workers in the production process is nowadays a real opportunity for our societies. In order to manage automata or to do computing works, a 65-year-old person can perfectly do the job, whereas the tasks carried out by machines in earlier times would have required younger workers under previous production techniques. The evolution of production techniques is thus also most favourable to the construction of a reverse retirement system.

In sum, these societal evolutions—a larger proportion of seniors in the population, as well as more healthy and more productive seniors—are such that, in the twenty-first-century economy, the construction of a reverse retirement system would no longer lead societies to low living standards and massive poverty, as this would have been the case during the longest part of history. Demographic and technological conditions in the early twenty-first century open a unique opportunity in history: a reverse retirement system is nowadays possible. But to what extent could such a system be effectively realized? Under which conditions could it be brought to existence? In order to answer these questions, we will now draw the main contours of a reverse retirement system, and enter into the details of its internal architecture.

[9] On the disconnection between the biological age and the chronological age, see Ponthiere (2017a).

4.2 Live, Live, Live

Compared to existing retirement systems, reverse retirement systems would differ on the ground that these would allow all young adults to enjoy a retirement period *before* they start working (and not only, as it is the case nowadays, *after* their entire career). Young beneficiaries of this retirement period would receive a pension allowance every month, without working. The main difference with respect to existing retirement systems would be that the beneficiaries of pensions would here be young adults, i.e., 'young pensioners'.

These young pensioners could then invest their free time in a myriad of possible activities. Possibly, they could invest in higher education, while being at the same time freed from the necessity to work. This would be a major achievement of reverse retirement systems to allow all young adults—not only the ones living in rich families—to attend higher education programmes without working.[10] The economic and social consequences of such a broader access to higher education would be substantial, not only in terms of what economists call human capital accumulation (accumulation of knowledge and skills), but, also, in terms of the participation of all citizens to the democratic life.

But higher education is not the only possible activity to be carried out during the initial period of retirement. Young pensioners could also invest their free time in the associative life (for instance, through benevolent work in NGOs), in the same way as senior retirees participate to associations nowadays. By redistributing the possibilities to live different lives, reverse retirement would not only reduce inequalities in education and skills, but, also, inequalities in the capacity to contribute the social good. Our young pensioners—whatever their family background is—could all become benefactors. Note also that there is a positive correlation between benevolent work (currently concentrated at senior ages) and higher education.[11]

[10] In France, about 550,000 adults aged between 18 and 25 do work during their higher education years. This concerns about 1 student out of 5 (data available at: https://www.education.gouv.fr/l-etat-de-l-ecole-2019-11246). About 770,000 students have a living standard that lies below the poverty line (sources: INSEE: *Enquête des revenus fiscaux et sociaux*). The COVID-19 pandemic has worsened that situation even more.

[11] See Prouteau (2018).

Under a reverse retirement system, pensions could also be used to allow young adults to settle as a family, and to give birth to a child, without having to wait the tenured labour contract that comes sometimes after a decade of precarious work.[12] This early opportunity to create a family goes against the current demographic trends: since the 1970s, the average age at motherhood (first child) has continuously increased: it has grown from about 24 years to about 30 years, in just a few decades.[13] This tendency towards the postponement of births is related to the increase in the duration of higher education. But besides the duration of studies, this trend has also been shown to be related to the impoverishment of labour careers for young adults. The young must take precarious short-term labour contracts over years and years before being tenured. The deterioration of the young's early working career explains also the postponement of the construction of a family. Note that nowadays, some young adults—those who benefit from the financial support of their parents—do not need to wait until age 30 to have their first child. The reverse retirement system would generalize that possibility of creating a family to the entire youth.

Generalizing the access to higher education, generalizing the participation to the associative life, generalizing the access to the family life. Reverse retirement systems would allow young adults to find their place in the society, and to invest their free time and their energy in things that really matter for them.

But nothing justifies restricting the uses of the initial retirement period to the previously mentioned activities. In the same way, as there exists no criterion for a good use of free time enjoyed by the senior retirees in our societies, there would be no criterion for a good use of free time for the young pensioners under a reverse retirement system. *Only one rule should prevail: live, live, live.*

A reverse retirement system aims at allowing citizens to insure themselves against the risk of having a short life. From that perspective, this insurance device pursues a unique goal: allowing persons to live as they want, in freedom and autonomy, as long as they are alive. Living life to the full, to celebrate the chance one has to exist. Living plainly in the present,

[12] Regarding the time period required before being tenured, see Viard (2019) in the case of France.

[13] On this tendency towards postponing births in European economies, see d'Albis et al. (2015).

without worrying about the possible occurrence of a future death. Some young pensioners would dedicate their free time to investment activities, i.e., activities oriented towards the future (e.g., education). But others would just enjoy watching the clouds pass in the sky.

Each person—and solely her—would decide how these early retirement years would be used. Early retirement should help young adults find the path towards personal flourishing. The mere fact of having to choose, at the beginning of young adulthood, how the retirement period will be lived can play a decisive role in the construction of a life. The early retirement period is like a blank canvas, an empty space that the person has to fill in. This early exercise of a choice of being oneself is a real challenge for human imagination. But this challenge is not useless. This gives each person the unique opportunity to see her life as a blank canvas open to all possible compositions.

4.3 On Financial Sustainability

In general, a retirement system is financially sustainable if and only if it brings some balance or equilibrium between revenues (i.e., pension contributions paid by workers) and expenditures (i.e., pension allowances paid to retirees).

The necessity to maintain a financial equilibrium has motivated a succession of reforms of pension systems since the 1990s in France and in Europe.[14] Population ageing, by increasing the number of retirees in comparison to the number of contributors, has caused a financial imbalance in retirement systems, because expenditures have grown more quickly than revenues.[15] During the last 40 years, the growth of wages (and contributions) has not been sufficient to balance the impact of population ageing. Moreover, the weak variations in fertility could not help finding some financial balance for pension systems.[16] Reforms of pension

[14] On these pension reforms, see Barr and Diamond (2008).

[15] To have an idea of the magnitude of the effects of ageing, and on the resulting financial imbalance of pension systems, let us take to figures from France. According to the INSEE, the number of contributors to pension systems in France was, in 1975, 3.2 larger than the number of retirees. Four decades later, the number of contributors is only 1.3 times the number of beneficiaries. See INSEE: *Tableaux de l'économie française, édition 2018*. https://www.insee.fr/fr/statistiques/3303437.

[16] During the Post-War baby boom, pay-as-you-go pension systems benefited of the Samuelson effect (also known as the intergenerational transfer effect): a rise in fertility

systems consisted in lengthening the period during which workers must contribute to the system, that is, these reforms consisted in postponing the effective retirement age. The goal was twofold: first, to increase the total amount of revenues for the pension system; second, to decrease the total amount of pension allowances paid to the retirees. The combination of larger revenues and smaller expenditures was supposed to bring the pension systems back to financial equilibrium, despite the imbalance caused by population ageing.[17]

This financial logic would also be present when considering a reverse retirement system. In order to be financially sustainable, such a system would have to exhibit some form of balance between revenues (contributions of workers) and expenditures (pension allowances paid to retirees). But there would be a major difference with respect to existing retirement systems: pension allowances would be paid not only to the elderly, but, also to young adults before they enter the labour market. On the revenues side, contributions would be paid by different subgroups of the population, the age of entrance on the labour market and the age of exit from work would be fixed at higher levels than in existing pension systems.

Would such a reverse pension system be financially sustainable? Several factors play a role in determining the financial viability of the system, exactly as for existing pension systems:

1. The age structure of the population and its dynamics;
2. The relation between age and labour productivity;
3. The ages of entrance and exit in the labour market.

This chapter will examine these three factors in detail.

4.4 Some Thought Experiments

In order to have an idea of the feasibility conditions of a reverse retirement system, let us proceed by carrying out some thought experiments.

increases, after 2 decades, the number of young adults (contributors to the system) with respect to the number of old adults (beneficiaries of the system). Population ageing has reduced the scope of the Samuelson effect, thus threatening the financial balance of pension systems. See Samuelson (1975).

[17] For instance, the rise of the effective retirement age has been achieved by increasing the legal number of contributing years required to have access to full pension rights.

This exercise is not about proposing an exhaustive study—with detailed numbers quantifying all variables at stake—of the financial feasibility of a reform consisting in reversing retirement systems at a given point in time, nor about providing a detailed assessment of its financial sustainability over time. On the contrary, the few numbers that we are going to present here aim only at allowing us to have an idea of the size of population groups concerned by such a reform, and of the constraints imposed by these groups on the form of a reverse retirement system.

As a first approximation, the (partial) reversal of pension systems can be presented as a reform that brings two major changes to existing (pay-as-you-go) pension systems: on the one hand, a postponement of the age of entrance in the labour market; on the other hand, a postponement of the age of (final) exit from the labour market. This double postponement modifies the number of contributors and the number of beneficiaries of pension systems. By postponing the age of entrance on the labour market, one reduces, within the groups of young adults, the number of contributors to the pension system, and one also increases the number of beneficiaries within these groups (the young pensioners). Moreover, by postponing the age of exit from the labour market, one increases the number of contributors among the seniors, and decreases the number of beneficiaries among old age groups. Quantifying the net variations in the numbers of contributors and beneficiaries induced by these changes constitutes a first step in the measurement of the financial consequences of reversing pension systems.[18]

Let us first start from existing pension systems, and consider the case of a fictitious postponement of the age of entrance and the age of exit from the labour market, everything else being left unchanged. What would be the effects, *ceteris paribus*, of this double postponement on the number of contributors and beneficiaries, and, hence, on the financial balance of pension systems?[19]

[18] Obviously, a reversal of pension systems would lead to several other changes—we will consider that point in more detail later on in this chapter—but as a first proxy, it is useful to focus on variations in the number of contributors and beneficiaries, everything else being left unchanged.

[19] It is only a simple thought experiment, which consists of displacing age groups across categories of contributors and beneficiaries. Later on in this chapter, we will consider the organization of the transition towards a reverse retirement system, a transition to be organized progressively along several years, in such a way as to divide the burden of the transition on a large number of successive cohorts (see infra).

Table 4.1 Numbers of contributors and beneficiaries, *Régime général des retraites*, France

Age groups	*Number of individuals*[a]	*Number of contributors*[b]	*Number of beneficiaries*[c]
18–20 years	2,403,034	1,027,776	0
21–23 years	2,263 657	1,287,584	0
24–25 years	1,478,647	927,387	0
…	…	…	…
62–64 years	2,414,383	352,365	1,577,956
65–67 years	2,385,773	147,008	2,052,820
68–69 years[d]	1,567,071	55,482	1,449,329

[a]These figures show the age structure of France on the 1st January 2018, men and women. *Source* CNAV, https://www.statistiques-recherches.cnav.fr/cotisants-au-regime-general.html
[b]These figures concern the number of contributors to the *Régime général* at the 31st December 2017. These are obtained by extrapolation from the distribution of the number of contributors by age for all pension regimes together, under the assumption that contributors to the *Régime général* account for 68.8% of all contributors. *Source* CNAV, https://www.statistiques-recherches.cnav.fr/cotisants-au-regime-general.html
[c]These figures concern the number of beneficiaries of a pension allowance from the *Régime général* at the 31st December 2017. *Source* CNAV, https://www.statistiques-recherches.cnav.fr/recueil-statistique-2017.html
[d]69 years included.

Answering that question is far from simple: if we take, for instance, the example of France, there exists not one, but a myriad of distinct pension systems. In order to provide a first answer, we will use the data of the *Caisse Nationale d'Assurance Vieillesse* (CNAV) that concern the *Régime de retraites général*, which covers about 8 workers out of 10.[20] Table 4.1 presents the size of different age groups, among the young and among the seniors (for year 2018), as well as the numbers of contributors and beneficiaries within these age groups.

Let us assume that a pension allowance is given to all persons aged between 18 and 20 years included, that is, during the first three years of adult life. In the light of the second column of Table 4.1, the number

[20] The *Régime général des retraites* includes about 18 million contributors, and about 14 million beneficiaries. The average monthly pension allowance is equal to about 700 euros, that is, about 50% of the average pension allowances (all regimes included), which is equal to about 1350 euros.

of young pensioners would be as high as 2.4 million persons, to whom pension allowances would be paid. But such a reform would also impose another cost, which consists of non-perceived pension contributions. By postponing the age of entrance on the labour market, the reform would lead to give up the contributions of about 1 million young individuals. If that reform involves also a postponement of the age of (final) retirement to 65 years, about 1.6 million seniors would leave the category of beneficiaries to enter the category of contributors.[21] In sum, if other aspects of the system were left unchanged, this reform would increase the total number of beneficiaries of pensions by about 800,000 persons, while the total number of contributors would increase by about 600,000 units. Based on these calculations, the ratio number of contributors over number of beneficiaries would fall, under that scenario, from 1.35 to 1.32.

A second thought experiment consists of considering the introduction of an initial retirement period between ages 18 and 23 (included) (6 years instead of 3 years). Under this more ambitious policy reform, the number of new young pensioners would be as high as 4.7 million, whereas the contributions of about 2.3 million young adults would vanish. In order to finance this reform within the pension system, the age of (final) retirement should be increased significantly. If the final retirement age is fixed to 65 years, only 1.6 million seniors would be added to the group of contributors, an insufficient number, which could not bring financial balance of the system. If, on the contrary, the retirement age was set to 68 years, about 3.6 million seniors would leave the group of beneficiaries and would enter the category of contributors.[22] At the end of the day, if the remaining of the pension system were left unchanged, the total number of beneficiaries would grow by about 1.1 million units, whereas the total number of contributors would increase by 1.3 million units, leading to a small decline in the ratio number of contributors over number of beneficiaries, from 1.35 to 1.34.

Despite all simplifying assumptions on which our calculations rely, these few thought experiments make appear the financial constraints that the age structure of the population imposes on any reform of (partial)

[21] We assume full employment of senior workers. Introducing senior unemployment would modify these figures, by reducing the number of contributors. If, for instance, the unemployment rate for seniors equals 10%, then only 1.4 million seniors would be added to the group of contributors to the pension system.

[22] Here again, we assume full employment of the seniors.

reversal of pension systems: *if one wants to avoid creating imbalance between the numbers of contributors and beneficiaries, one can only give a pension to young retirees provided the final age of exit from work is sufficiently postponed.* The longer the initial retirement period is, the larger the postponement of the final retirement age should be. The age of entrance and the age of exit from the labour market are thus two pivotal ages of a reverse retirement system. These two pivotal ages are related to each other through the requirement of financial balance of the pension system.[23]

Although these few thought experiments give some ideas of the effects of a reversal of pension systems on the numbers of contributors and beneficiaries, these leave several questions unanswered.[24] Their main limitation is to focus on the counting of beneficiaries and contributors within the reformed pension system, without telling us anything regarding the amounts of the pension paid to retirees, and the amounts of contributions. These two parameters are key components of any balanced reform of pension systems.

4.5 A Basic Pension or More?

At which level should we set the pension allowance paid to young pensioners? At the level of the average pension under the *Régime général des retraites*, that is, 700 euros? Or, alternatively, at the level of the minimum wage (1,280 euros)? Or at the average level of pensions in France, all pension regimes included (1,360 euros)?

If our calculations are correct, it is possible to include a set of young pensioners in pension systems without modifying significantly the ratio number of contributors over number of beneficiaries provided the age of exit from the labour market is sufficiently increased. This (quasi) constancy of the ratio contributors/beneficiaries suggests that it could be possible to give to each young retiree a monthly pension allowance

[23] Our analysis abstracts also from another potential effect of the reform: the jobs left by young workers could be potentially taken by older workers who were previously in unemployment. But this bonus effect is far from automatic, and looks more like a second-order effect. Moreover, the main objective of the pension reversal reform is to construct an insurance against a short life, and not a reduction of unemployment rate.

[24] This analysis is purely static. We will consider intertemporal aspects of the reform later on in this chapter.

equal or close to the average pension allowance given to the entire set of retirees, that is, between 1,300 and 1,400 euros.[25]

But the level of the pension allowance given to young pensioners constitutes a political choice, about which various rival positions could be defended. These positions should be debated and assessed collectively by citizens. The reverse retirement system raises lots of trade-offs of political nature, which cannot be solved by the expert alone, but which should be submitted to democratic deliberations. Only (open) public debates could lead to a precise drawing of the contours of the reverse retirement system, and of the horizons that it opens for the youth.

The most important element to be taken into account consists of the general form that one wants to give to the reverse retirement system. The generosity of the system is two-dimensional: on the one hand, the—more or less long—duration of the initial retirement period, and, on the other hand, the—more or less high—level of the monthly pension allowance given to each young adult. Do we prefer a long retirement period, but with a basic pension allowance (between 700 and 1,000 euros per month)? Or, alternatively, a shorter retirement period, but associated with a more comfortable pension (about 1,300 euros per month)?

Given that the funding of the reverse retirement system relies heavily on the labour of senior workers, a key dimension of a reform consisting in a reversal of pension systems concerns the—acceptable—postponement of the final age of exit from the labour market: 65 years, 67 years or even 69 years? The more or less high level of the final retirement age affects directly the generosity of the reverse retirement system, concerning both the length of the initial retirement period and the level of pension allowances given to the young.

In the light of all this, the construction of a reverse retirement system cannot be made without a public debate including all generations (young and old), because all generations are linked together within the system of social insurance against the risk of a short life. This is not about making generations compete with each other for larger allowances and more leisure time, but, rather, about constructing a dialogue between

[25] One should notice that the stability of the ratio contributors/beneficiaries is only a necessary condition, but not a sufficient condition for preserving the financial equilibrium of pension systems. As we shall see, a more detailed study of the feasibility of reverse retirement would require also to considering various scenarios relative to the revenues' side of the system, concerning the levels of contributions and the distribution of these.

generations, in order to think collectively about the relations between the different ages of life. The final goal would be to draw collectively new links between generations who, taken together, make the society.

Beyond discussions about the duration of the initial retirement period, the amount of pension allowances and the retirement age for the seniors, a democratic debate about a reverse retirement system should also address another key issue: the funding of social protection. Which taxes and contributions? For which social protection in the twenty-first century? We touch here a general issue that goes far beyond the topic of the present essay. But this issue is inevitably raised once one considers the construction of a new pillar of the welfare state.[26]

4.6 Demographic and Technological Evolutions

How sustainable is a system of reverse retirement? Could it be sustainable in a world where age structures of populations vary, and where production technologies change continuously?

Let us first examine the sustainability issue from a demographic perspective, by considering the long-run dynamics of age structures, for the case of the French economy.[27] In order to reverse retirement systems, two age groups are particularly relevant: on the one hand, the group of young adults (aged between 18 and 25 years), which includes the new beneficiaries of the reformed pension system; on the other hand, the group of young seniors (aged between 62 and 69 years), which includes the new contributors to the reverse pension system. Table 4.2 presents the evolution of these two age groups on the basis of long-run forecasts by INSEE, up to year 2070.[28]

[26] This question includes the setting of a just funding of pension allowances through contributions whose burden is fairly distributed among the population. But this issue goes beyond the mere discussion on pensions, and concerns also the design of a just system of social protection against all risks (not only the risk of a short life), as well as the contours of a just fiscal system. We cannot examine all these issues here, but this does not make these issues less urgent from the perspective of social justice (see Fleurbaey et al. 2016; Leroux et al. 2021).

[27] Note that the dynamics of the age structure matters for the financial equilibrium of all pension systems in general. On this, see Blanchet (2007).

[28] These forecasts are based on several assumptions: first, a total fertility rate equals to 1.95 children per women; second, a period life expectancy at birth that grows until

Table 4.2 Demographic forecasts, 2040 and 2070, France

Age groups	*Number of persons in 2018*[a]	*Number of persons in 2040*[b]	*Number of persons in 2070*[c]
(1) 18–20 years	2,403,034	2,464,540	2,514,676
(2) 21–23 years	2,263,657	2,387,290	2,443,649
(3) 24–25 years	1,478,647	1,595,079	1,612,829
…	…	…	…
(4) 62–64 years	2,414,383	2,392,205	2,661,389
(5) 65–67 years	2,385,773	2,588,284	2,565,091
(6) 68–69 years	1,567,071	1,712,824	1,719,085
Ratio $\left[\frac{(1)+(2)+(3)}{(4)+(5)+(6)}\right]$	0,968	0,963	0,946

[a] Data from CNAV: https://www.statistiques-recherches.cnav.fr/cotisants-au-regime-general.html
[b] Forecasts by INSEE: https://www.insee.fr/fr/statistiques/2524484
[c] Forecasts by INSEE: https://www.insee.fr/fr/statistiques/2524484

From the perspective of the financial sustainability of a reverse retirement system, the figures presented in Table 4.2 are somewhat reassuring: the age structure will evolve in the next 50 years, but the relative proportion of young adults (with respect to young seniors) will not increase. This proportion is also expected to fall slightly in relative terms. The general tendency towards a lower mortality—and the associated lengthening of life—is favourable for a sustainable system of reverse retirement.

One could reply to this that INSEE forecasts used in Table 4.2 are based on hypotheses relative to the long-run dynamics of fertility and mortality, and that nothing guarantees the validity of these hypotheses once a reverse retirement system would have been introduced. For instance, if the payment of a pension allowance to young adults leads to some fertility rebound (a new baby boom), forecasts on Table 4.2 would not be valid any more, and the (relative) proportion of young retirees could increase. In other words, the introduction of a reverse retirement system could generate behavioural reactions that threaten the financial sustainability of the system over the long run.[29]

Such behavioural responses to a policy change are hardly predictable. However, one can conjecture that these are, over the long period, only a second-order factor in comparison to a more powerful long-run trend: the generalized improvement of the health status of seniors and the associated falling trend of mortality, which are both corollaries of medical and scientific progress. The decline of mortality over the long run reveals the improvement of the health status of individuals at given ages. Seniors are in a better health today than in the past, which makes it possible for them to work longer, at ages that could not have been considered previously. The growing disconnection between the chronological age and the biological age constitutes the main demographic trend making the reversal of pension systems not only possible in the short run, but, also, sustainable in the long run.[30]

reaching 93 years for women and 90 years for men; third, a yearly net migration of 40,000 units. See: https://www.insee.fr/fr/statistiques/2524484.

[29] In a similar manner, it was argued that the introduction of a classical pay-as-you-go pension system causes a fall of fertility, which threatens the financial equilibrium of that system. See Zhang et al. (2001).

[30] On this disconnection between the chronological age and the biological age, see Ponthiere (2017a).

Other evolutions, of technological nature, are also likely to make the reversal of pension systems sustainable in the long period. As we have seen, our economies shifted, across centuries, from production techniques that were labour-intensive—and requiring a highly physical labour—to more capital-intensive techniques of production, where capital—machines, computers, automata—have reduced the requirements in terms of physical force and body resilience for workers.

This long-run evolution of production techniques could explain, in part, the more or less stable relation that is observed between the labour productivity and the age of workers. This relationship is not simple to quantify, because labour productivity is *multidimensional*. It is possible that, as a person becomes older, some skills depreciate (e.g., physical strength), whereas other skills improve (e.g., sociability).[31] Moreover, the relation between labour productivity and the age of workers is *bidirectional*: an employer who anticipates that his employee will retire may be tempted to stop investing in the continued formation of the worker, which yields indeed a fall of productivity with age, but which is not due to the age of the worker, but to the employer's behaviour. Taking these difficulties into account, empirical studies tried to quantify the relation between the age of workers and labour productivity. Their results are mixed.[32] Some studies conclude that the productivity profile is growing with age, but stabilizes around age 50. Other studies, on the contrary, show that the productivity profile has an inverted U shape: labour productivity would increase until a certain age, and, then, would fall.[33] But despite the absence of consensus across empirical studies, it can be concluded that there exists probably no sharp decline of labour productivity beyond age 60.

It should be stressed here that existing empirical studies have measured labour productivity along an age interval that covers actual careers, and, as such, have not explored the evolution of labour productivity above age 65. From the perspective of studying the feasibility and sustainability of reverse pension systems, this constitutes an obvious limitation, since

[31] See Van Ours and Stoeldraijer (2010).

[32] See the survey of Skirbekk (2004).

[33] On the basis of French statistics, Aubert and Crepon (2003) rejected the null hypothesis of older workers being less productive than younger workers. According to these authors, labour productivity grows continuously until age 40, then grows very slowly until age 50, and finally stabilizes.

the age interval between 65 and 70 is precisely the key age interval in which the extra work of seniors would be needed to finance the pension allowances paid to the young. However, one can make the conjecture that the relative importance of physical labour will keep on decreasing in the next decades. Jointly with the continuous improvement of senior health status, this hypothesis leads to the plausible scenario of a (quasi) stable labour productivity between ages 65 and 70.

In sum, expected future demographic and technological changes appear to be favourable to the construction and maintenance of reverse retirement systems. Nevertheless, such a policy reform is not marginal: this is not about changing only one parameter in a pension system, but, rather, about changing the whole philosophy of a pension system, in order to make it serve the ideal of insurance against the risk of a short life. The associated changes—the introduction of an initial retirement period before the career, the postponement of the age of final exit from work—are far from minor changes. As such, that non-marginal pension reform is likely to raise lots of oppositions. The remainder of this chapter examines the main criticisms against the construction of a reverse retirement system.

4.7 Reward and Free Lunch

As we have seen, the question of social justice lies at the very heart of the justification of a reversal of pension systems. Reversing pension system constitutes a reform allowing to reconciling the universal uncertainty about the length of life and concerns for social justice. But there exists no unique conception of social justice, and one way to attack reverse retirement systems may consist of adopting alternative normative foundations, which lay a weaker emphasis on issues of compensation, and a stronger emphasis on reward and merit.[34]

The retirement period is often perceived as a kind of reward for a long career. Workers deserve their retirement, because they have worked 35 or 40 years, or even more. From that perspective, the retirement period should only be given to workers who deserve it, i.e., to these who have, by their efforts, contributed long enough to the life and prosperity of the society. If one adopts the view of retirement as a reward, the reversal of

[34] On that criticism, see Ponthiere (2020b).

retirement systems is unacceptable. Actually, under a reverse retirement system, young adults would benefit from a pension allowance *without having worked previously*. Thus, retirement would no longer be a reward, something that one has to deserve.

Under a reverse pension system, it is possible that, in some cases, several individuals would benefit from a pension allowance without *ever* working in their life. This particular case arises when some persons die prematurely before having reached the first pivotal age, i.e., the age of entrance in the labour market. Under a reverse retirement system, these individuals would benefit from pension allowances without any labour (past or future): a real *free lunch*.

Can retirement systems leading to free lunches be socially desirable? Or should we, in the light of these free lunches, give up reverse retirement systems, and consider other reforms?[35]

In order to deal with that criticism, it should first be stressed that the beneficiaries of a free lunch under a reverse retirement system are persons who belong to a specific group: these are the unlucky persons who suffer from a premature death, which prevents them from reaching the age when they would have started to work. However, as we have seen in Chapter 2, the harm due to a premature death is substantial: an early death cancels all life plans, all dreams, without any possibility of future achievements for these persons. The free lunch that these unlucky persons receive can thus be defended as a kind of reparation for the serious harms suffered by these persons. Only extremely disadvantaged persons would thus receive such a free lunch, which can be interpreted as a fair compensation.

The injustice caused by the existence of a free lunch for some persons should not be considered in absolute terms, but should be compared with the injustice caused by a short life for these persons. These two injustices should be weighed against each other, in order to determine on which side the injustice is the most salient. Arguing that the reverse retirement system involves a free lunch is not sufficient to disqualify such a pension system. One should demonstrate that the injustice caused by the existence

[35] A possibility of compromise between the goals of (i) caring about the short-lived and (ii) avoiding free lunches could consist in keeping standard pension systems (without initial retirement period), but postponing the age of exit from the labour market, in order to reduce contributions paid by the young (i.e., the potentially short-lived), and transfer as much money as possible to the young. This second-best road—where the state does not use the age of entrance on the labour market as a policy instrument—is explored in Fleurbaey et al. (2016).

of free lunches is more substantial than the injustice caused by a short life. This proof is hard to provide.

These concerns make us defend the system of reverse retirement. True, there is probably something unfair in the existence of free lunches: it does not seem fair to give pension allowances to persons who never worked in their whole life, and who may not work at all. But we think that the harm caused by a premature death consists of an even more severe form of social injustice. The larger injustice faced by the unlucky short-lived should be acknowledged, and the victims of these injustices should definitely have priority over others. *The free lunch enjoyed by the persons who die prematurely constitutes nothing else than the price to pay for the construction of an effective social insurance against the risk of a short life*.

4.8 Careers and Incentives

A second criticism concerns the possible consequences of a reversal of retirement systems: this policy reform might provide inadequate incentives to individuals, and discourage them from investing time and efforts in tasks necessary for a good functioning of the society. By distorting the incentive structure of the economy, the shift to a reverse retirement system could potentially threaten the prosperity of the society.

Any society is based on institutions—what Douglas North called 'scaffolding'—that determine the rules of the game, that is, the form that interactions between members of the society take.[36] Rules dictated by institutions provide incentives to individuals (e.g., incentives to work, to study, etc.). By providing these incentives, institutions influence the behaviours of individuals, and the activities in which they invest time and energy.

Like all institutions, the existing retirement system provides incentives. It encourages individuals to study, since the level of pension allowances is generally based on the wage, which is often increasing with the education level. The existing pension system also encourages individuals to work during long decades, in such a way as to have access to full pension rights once retired.

[36] See North (2005).

What would these incentives to study and to work become under a reverse retirement system? Would the reversal of pension systems make our societies converge to the 'end of work'?[37]

The effects of a reversal of retirement systems on the incentive structure are hard to forecast and to quantify. At this stage of history, no welfare state has ever introduced a reverse retirement system. In the absence of any example, it is extremely difficult to anticipate the potential effects of this policy reform. Forecasting difficulties are especially substantial in the case of the introduction of a reverse retirement system, since this major institutional change may have not only quantitative effects (i.e., changes concerning the levels of economic and social outcomes), but, also, may lead to major qualitative effects (i.e., changes in the form of relations between economic and social variables). Institutional changes can lead to what Oded Galor calls *regime shifts*: this can make an economy shift from an economic regime to another regime, each regime being characterized by its own laws and regularities.[38] When an economic regime changes, the shape of relations between variables is affected. A regime shift coincides with a major change in the functioning of societies and in their dynamics.

Given the possibility of such a regime shift (indirectly) induced by the introduction of a reverse retirement system, it is extremely difficult to forecast the long-run effects of this policy reform. At this stage, we can only provide some clues, but no definitive answer.

Let us consider the issue of incentives to work. Could the introduction of a reverse retirement system weaken incentives to work, and lead to the 'end of work'?

One can have serious doubts about this. First of all, the construction of a reverse retirement system would not necessarily imply a reduction of the working time, because it would lead to both postponing the age of entrance in the labour market and the age of exit from the labour market. Reversing pension systems does not mean to reduce the quantity of hours

[37] The influential book *The End of Work* by Jeremy Rifkin announced, in the mid-1990s, the end of industrial jobs because of technological advances. But the 'end of work' is here of a different nature: the question is to know whether the reversal of retirement systems would not cause the emergence of a society where the incentives to work would be so low that the aggregate quantity of labour would reach too low levels, thus questioning the prosperity—if not the survival—of the society.

[38] On regime shifts, see Galor (2011).

worked, but just to allocate the working time in a different way along the life cycle, in such a way as to insure citizens against the risk of a short life.

When looking at history, we can see that some previous episodes of postponement of the entrance on the labour market took place, without generating disincentives to work. The best historical example is the abolishment of child labour in Europe at the end of the nineteenth century and the beginning of the twentieth century. The abolishment of child labour did not weaken incentives to work in the society as a whole. Nor did this reform disqualify the culture of work. On the contrary, during the twentieth century, the output growth has been higher than ever before in history. In the light of that example, it is exaggerated to believe that the postponement of the entrance on the labour market by a few years (because of the introduction of an initial retirement period) would suffice to cause a serious economic crisis and to lead our societies to the end of work. One should also remind that the effective average age of entrance on the labour market is nowadays equal to about 23 years in France.[39] Hence, the construction of a reverse retirement system would only consist of accompanying—and encouraging—an existing trend. The tendency towards more years spent in higher education is already at work, and generalizing the access of all young adults to higher education would encourage this even more, while, at the same time, reduce inequalities in human capital levels.

Another argument supporting reverse retirement is based on the concept of trust. Actually, providing to all young adults an initial retirement period allowing them to find their personal path in life reveals all the trust that the society places in the youth. By its mere existence, this system demonstrates that each young person's life matters, and matters as such. *A reverse retirement system sends a signal to members of young generations, showing them that their life is not a means to achieve some external social goal, but, rather, is regarded as an end in itself.* Thus, the introduction of a reverse retirement system would allow a society to provide collectively a proof, by means of a kind of signal, of all the trust it places in young generations. The social consequences of such a signal sent by earlier generations to all young individuals may be substantial, because signals of trust are often followed by marks of loyalty: individuals who were the subject of trust in the past generally provide extra efforts to give

[39] Sources: INSEE.

back what was invested in them.[40] From that perspective, the introduction of a reverse retirement system would make our societies enter the era of trust, with all positive consequences it can have.[41]

Let us now consider the incentives to study. In our societies, higher education has a double cost: on the one hand, higher education has an explicit cost (registration fees, books, etc.), and, on the other hand, it also has an implicit or hidden cost: all wages that the student must give up because of the time spent studying rather than working. This second cost is called the opportunity cost of studying: the time spent studying cannot be spent working, and this constitutes a substantial—but hidden—cost of attending higher education.

Under a reverse retirement system, the opportunity cost of higher education would vanish, because paid labour would not concern the young pensioners any more.[42] By cancelling the opportunity cost of higher education, a reverse retirement system would encourage young persons to invest even more in higher education. This new incentive structure would thus lead to encourage human capital accumulation even more. This incentive effect would, jointly with the access effect studied earlier (the possibility for young adults from poor families to invest also in higher education), definitely reinforce the human capital accumulation in our societies. Thus, incentives to study would not be weakened, but, rather, would be reinforced by the introduction of a reverse retirement system.

[40] See the game theoretical literature on trust games (sequential prisoners' dilemma), where a first-mover player must choose how much to invest in a second player, who decides, in a second stage, how much to give back to the first mover. In out context, the first-mover is made of earlier generations, and the second-movers are young generations. A reverse retirement system can be interpreted as a trust signal sent by the first-mover, which will encourage the loyalty of second-mover players (young generations), under the form of a higher amount given back to earlier generations. On trust games, see Berg et al. (1995).

[41] The positive effects of trust on the economy were first underlined by John Stuart Mill, in his *Principles of Political Economy* (see Mill 1848).

[42] Note that young adults who still want to work could, under that retirement system, work benevolently. But even in that case, the monetary opportunity cost of higher education is weakened.

4.9 An Effective Insurance Against a Short Life?

Although it is attractive in theory, the reversal of retirement systems may face some serious operationalization problems in practice. Could it be really sufficient to provide to citizens a social insurance against the risk of a short life? The answer is: No. Reverse retirement is not sufficient to construct a social insurance against a premature death. Other public policies are necessary in order to make such insurance really effective.

Let us first consider the question of the *effective* access to higher education. The pension allowance paid to all young adults would allow them to invest more free time in higher education only if the higher education system has a sufficiently large capacity to welcome all young individuals. Under strong capacity constraints, the introduction of a reverse retirement system would not really allow young adults to invest more time in higher education. Actually, reversing pension systems could increase congestion in higher education programmes even more, and, hence, have the paradoxical effect of discouraging higher education. Hence, the construction of a real social insurance against the risk of a short life requires to increase the capacity of higher education institutions, to really allow all young adults to find the path of their flourishing, their place in the society.

Other factors may threaten the effectiveness of a social insurance against a short life. Actually, the existence of a bias towards the future may encourage young pensioners to save a large part of their pension allowance for their old days. This behavioural response would definitely go against the ideal of a social insurance against a short life: if resources sent to the young age are mechanically transferred back to the old age, this will prevent the good functioning of an insurance against a premature death. The reason is the following: in case of a premature death, the amount saved is lost. Hence, from the perspective of a short-lived person, it would have been definitely better not to have saved these amounts of money. Of course, no one can anticipate one's premature death, and this is precisely the reason why a reverse retirement system aims at forcing individuals to enjoy a retirement period and pension allowances when young, that is, when being still alive. Behavioural responses may counterbalance the reverse retirement system, and make the insurance against a premature death ineffective. As a consequence, the construction of a social insurance against a short life requires to introducing taxes and transfers that discourage the reallocation of resources towards older ages.[43] These fiscal instruments are a necessary complement of the reverse retirement system in the presence of a bias towards the future. Without these, the insurance against a short life would remain ineffective.

Another factor limiting the scope of an insurance against a short life is the poor quality of the natural environment. How could young pensioners—and, hence, the unlucky short-lived—flourish in a highly polluted world? Is the payment of a mere pension allowance every month sufficient to really allow for the compensation for a short life? This answer is, here again: No. The pollution of the air, of the water and of soils causes a large number of premature deaths, and leads to substantial harms for the persons who have a short life. As a consequence, a reverse retirement system offering a pension to all young adults is not sufficient to really allow for a compensation of the short-lived. The construction of a social insurance against a short life thus invites also policies aimed at reducing the pollution of the natural environment. Obviously, there exist many other good reasons to justify such environmental policies (e.g., intergenerational justice), but the construction of a social insurance against a short life reinforces, under general conditions, the urgency of a more ambitious environmental policy, by providing an extra justification for these interventions.[44]

In sum, these few criticisms are well-founded, but these do not suffice to question the principle of reversing retirement systems. What these criticisms highlight is merely that the realization of an effective social insurance against a short life requires, in addition to the reversal of retirement systems, a set of adequate public policies making that insurance fully effective.

4.10 Organizing the Transition

Another major difficulty remains to be addressed: the transition from existing retirement systems to reverse retirement systems. The transition problem comes from the fact that many cohorts of persons have already

[43] On the optimal taxation of saving in the context of unequal longevities, see Fleurbaey et al. (2014).

[44] On this issue, see Ponthiere (2017b).

worked during long decades without having benefited, at the beginning of adulthood, of any initial retirement period. It is thus difficult to ask to these cohorts of workers to postpone the time at which they will retire for the sake of funding the initial retirement period of new young pensioners under a reverse retirement system. How could one solve the transition problem?

A first thing to notice is that the transition from a standard retirement system towards a reverse retirement system cannot take place in a decentralized manner, that is, on the sole basis of individual decisions. A coordination action by the state is necessary for such a transition. Otherwise, in the case of a fully decentralized transition left to the free will of individuals, there is a risk of seeing the economy collapse, because of a shortage of workers.[45] To see this, note first that, under a fully decentralized transition, senior workers would not accept to work beyond the retirement age prevailing under the old, standard, pension system. But young adults, at the same time, would like to benefit from the initial retirement period proposed by the new reverse retirement system. As a consequence, during the time of the transition, both young adults and senior adults would not accept to work, both groups wanting to enjoy a retirement period (for different reasons). Thus, the production of goods and services would rely on a too narrow segment of the active population (i.e., in age of working). Hence, in the case of a decentralized transition, the level of living standards would fall almost mechanically. Depending on how the pivotal ages of pension systems are fixed, this fall of living standards might, in the worse cases, turn into a collapse of the economy.

In order to avoid this undesirable outcome, there has to be a coordination organized by the state. Public authorities have a key role to play in order to organize a progressive transition towards a reverse retirement system. This transition consists of increasing progressively the age of entrance on the labour market (thus the duration of the initial retirement period) and the age of final exit from the labour market. Only such a progressive change can insure a smooth transition from standard retirement to reverse retirement. A smooth transition can be achieved by requiring, at the time of the transition, that young adults benefit only of a short initial retirement period (which could, for instance, increase by two months every year), while imposing, at the same time, senior

[45] On the organization of this transition, see Ponthiere (2020b).

workers to retire a bit later on every year (for instance, three more months of work every year). By adopting this progressive process, one could smoothly increase the duration of the initial retirement period—and secure its funding—by increasing progressively the age of entrance and the age of exit on the labour market.

Organizing a smooth transition across a large number of cohorts would exhibit a double virtue. On the one hand, this smoothing of the transition from standard retirement to reverse retirement would allow the economy to avoid a risk of serious contraction, due to a too low quantity of labour (i.e., a too narrow segment of the active population that is effectively at work during the transition). On the other hand, by a smoothing effect, this would better divide the burden of the transition among generations. The larger the number of generations involved in the transition is, and the weaker is the burden to be faced by each generation of workers.[46]

The cost of the transition towards a reverse retirement system can be even more reduced when the age structure of the population is more favourable to the transition, that is, when the cohorts of senior workers are larger than the cohorts of young adults. Interestingly, the age pyramid in France and in other European countries is currently favourable to the organization of this transition, because it still exhibits the traces of the Post-War baby boom. More precisely, cohorts of persons aged between 50 and 75 years are of large sizes. One can thus use this trait of contemporary populations to better organize the transition towards reverse retirement. Thanks to their large size, the cohorts of baby boomers can collectively share the burden of the transition, without having to bear too large costs at the individual level. The age structure in the early twenty-first century is most favourable for a transition towards reverse retirement.

4.11 An Alternative to Other Reforms?

Could reverse retirement do better than other reforms of the welfare state, such as a basic income reform, or a universal capital endowment?

Let us first consider a classical of the reform of social protection: the introduction of a universal basic income.[47] A universal basic income

[46] Transition issues are not specific to reverse retirement systems, but occur each time we consider a change of pension system. See Masson (2003).

[47] See Van Parijs and Vanderborght (2018).

would have the virtue to favour the autonomy of individuals. By providing a solid alternative to work, a basic income would also increase the bargaining power of workers when facing employers. Moreover, by being unconditional, the basic income could also simplify the functioning of social insurance, by replacing lots of allowances systems that are hard to manage.

One could interpret reverse retirement as a device that provides an unconditional allowance to all young adults, a kind of basic income for the young.[48] However, there exists a fundamental difference between the basic income reform and the reverse retirement: whereas the first is truly universal, and provides an income to everyone, the second *conditions* the granting of the pension allowance to the age of citizens. This difference is rooted in the goal pursued by a reverse retirement system: the ultimate end is to insure citizens against the risk of a short life. The insurance logic requires to concentrating the 'good things of life' at young ages and the 'bad things of life' at older ages. A system of basic income treats all individuals in a symmetric manner, whatever their age is, and, as such, is not in line with the logic of a social insurance against a short life.[49]

A second, major difference, concerns the funding of these two policy reforms. Regarding the funding of the basic income, various sources were proposed, such as, for instance, the introduction of a tax on polluting energy (see Genet and Van Parijs).[50] The introduction of a basic income would require either to introduce new taxes, or to raise the level of existing taxes. On the contrary, a reverse retirement system includes, in its proper functioning, the sources of funding for the pension allowances paid to young pensioners: the mandatory contributions paid by senior workers maintained at work in the new retirement system.

[48] As such, the reverse retirement system could serve also as a substitute for numerous devices targeting the citizens aged 25 or less, such as, in France, the 'RSA jeune' (basic income), the 'Garantie Jeune' (housing), the aid for the driving licence, etc.

[49] Note that, to the extent that a universal basic income could improve the situation of the young—and, hence, of short-lived persons—this reform could be defended as a second-best device serving, in a world where policy instruments are limited, the ideal of an insurance against a short life. But it should be stressed that this reform would only be a second-best policy, whose effects on the injustice faced by the short-lived would be far less substantial than the ones induced by a reverse retirement reform.

[50] See Genet and Van Parijs (1992).

Let us now compare reverse retirement with alternative policy devices targeting the youth, such as the Danish system of monthly education vouchers studied by Cecile Van de Velde, or the project-stipend proposed by Jean Viard.[51] Monthly education vouchers (distributed during 72 months, conditionally on resources) allow all young individuals to have access to higher education. Viard's project-stipend generalizes this kind of device to other forms of learning (possibly informal learning). The underlying idea is to give to each young person aged between 16 and 28 years an allowance (reduced by 50% in case of extra labour earnings), in order to allow her to make the four fundamental learnings of life—studying, working, travelling and building an affective life—necessary to be prepared to an adult life in the modern society.

Reverse retirement shares with these alternative policy devices a key feature: this is targeted towards the youth (contrary to the basic income studied above). But a fundamental divergence is worth being underlined: whereas monthly education vouchers and the project-stipend are *conditional* on the young adult being invested in some form of learning process (either formal or informal), a reverse retirement system would give to each young adult a pension allowance *without any required counterpart*. As we have seen, the goal pursued by reverse retirement is not to prepare young individuals to anything, but, more basically, to insure themselves against the risk of having a short life. The underlying philosophy is thus here to insure citizens, and not to prepare them or to include them in the society.

Let us now examine another policy proposal: the introduction of a universal capital endowment (universal inheritance), paid once, at the beginning of adult life. This policy reform, proposed by Bruce Ackerman and Anne Alstott, has recently received attention in the works of economists such as Anthony Atkinson and Thomas Piketty.[52] It consists in paying to each young adult a minimal inheritance. According to Piketty, this universal capital endowment could be equal to 60% of the average wealth, that is, about 120,000 euros. This capital endowment could be given to each citizen at the age of 25 years. The goal pursued by a universal capital endowment is to reduce inequalities in wealth across families, and to offer to each citizen some equal opportunities in life.

[51] See Van de Velde (2008) and Viard (2019).

[52] See Ackerman and Alstott (1999), as well as Atkinson (2015) and Piketty (2019).

The funding of this policy reform would be obtained by a heavy taxation of inheritance, in the spirit of John Stuart Mill's pioneer work.[53]

Being targeted exclusively towards young adults, the universal capital endowment device shares some important characteristics with the reverse retirement system. However, two important divergences should be underlined. First, the logics underlying these two devices differ. Whereas the universal capital endowment (universal inheritance) aims at reducing the effects of wealth inequalities across families, the reverse retirement device aims at lowering the well-being inequalities due to unequal longevities across individuals. These two policy reforms thus attack distinct injustices, which makes these complementary. Second, one should also distinguish between the consequences of these two policy reforms. Both policy devices allow their young beneficiaries to pursue their life goals while being freed from material constraints. But the universal inheritance device has also the effect of transforming its beneficiaries in wealth managers, a paradoxical implication of that policy.[54]

Finally, the reverse retirement system can also be compared with other policy devices proposing other ways to divide, at the scale of the human life cycle, the available time between work, leisure, family life and other activities, as the device of extended social security (*sécurité sociale étendue*) proposed by Alain Supiot.[55] The extended social security aims at giving to all workers more freedom and autonomy in the organization of their career, and of their life in general. This is about allowing workers to take sabbatical leave when they want. Extended social security systems would thus introduce more flexibility in the relation of workers with their job, and would allow them to making the rhythm of their professional career better coincide with their personal rhythms.

In some cases, the extended social security system could have implications that are close to the ones of a reverse retirement system. Actually, if young adults choose to take a sabbatical leave at the very beginning of

[53] In his *Principles of Political Economy*, John Stuart Mill defended a 100% rate of taxation of all inheritance beyond some critical threshold, in such a way as to give to all young individuals the same basic endowment of wealth, allowing them to start their life in autonomy.

[54] We are back here to past debates about the best periodicity for the payment of a universal basic income: a regular monthly flow of income *versus* a wealth stock paid once and for all at the beginning of adulthood. See Van Parijs and Vanderborght (2018).

[55] See Supiot (1999).

their career, the resulting situation would be close to the one prevailing under reverse retirement. However, as we have seen, the presence of cognitive biases—the denial of death and the bias towards the future—is so widespread that few young adults would, under an extended social security scheme, choose the reverse retirement option (that is, an early sabbatical leave). Moreover, the extended social security pursues goals that are different from the ones associated with reverse retirement. The extended social security aims at favouring a better conciliation of professional and personal lives. Its goal is thus not to insure citizens against the risk of a short life. An extended social security system could thus reach its goal of larger flexibility for workers, but it could not, under general conditions, achieve a reduction of the harm caused by a premature death.

References

Ackerman, Bruce, and Anne Alstott. 1999. *The Stakeholder Society*. New Haven: Yale University Press.

Atkinson, Anthony. 2015. *Inequality: What Can Be Done?* Cambridge, MA: Harvard University Press.

Aubert, Patrick, and Bruno Crépon. 2003. 'La productivité des salariés âgés: Une tentative d'estimation'. *Economie Et Prévisions* 368: 95–119.

Barr, Nicholas, and Peter Diamond. 2008. *Reforming Pensions*. Oxford: Oxford University Press.

Berg, Joyce, John Dickhaut, and Kevin McCabe. 1995. 'Trust, Reciprocity, and Social History'. *Games and Economic Behaviour* 10: 122–142.

Blanchet, Didier. 2007. 'Perspectives démographiques et marché du travail: quelle relation?' In *Les retraites: libres opinions d'experts européens*, edited by F. Legros. Paris: Economica.

D'Albis, Hippolyte, Angela Greulich, and Gregory Ponthiere. 2015. *Avoir un enfant plus tard. Enjeux sociodémographiques du report des naissances*. Paris: Editions rue d'Ulm.

Fleurbaey, Marc, Marie-Louise Leroux, Pierre Pestieau, and Gregory Ponthiere. 2016. 'Fair Retirement Under Risky Lifetime'. *International Economic Review* 57: 177–210.

Fleurbaey, Marc, Marie-Louise Leroux, and Gregory Ponthiere. 2014. 'Compensating the Dead'. *Journal of Mathematical Economics* 51: 28–41.

Galor, Oded. 2011. *Unified Growth Theory*. Princeton: Princeton University Press.

Genet, Michel, and Philippe Van Parijs. 1992. 'Eurogrant'. *Basic Income Research Group Bulletin* 15: 4–7.

Lee, Ronald. 2003. 'The Demographic Transition: Three Centuries of Fundamental Change'. *Journal of Economic Perspectives* 17: 167–190.
Leroux, Marie-Louise, Pierre Pestieau, and Gregory Ponthiere. 2021. 'Fair Long Term Care Insurance'. *Social Choice and Welfare* 57: 503–533.
Masson, André. 2003. 'Redistribution et équité intergénérationnelle'. In *Epargne, assurance-vie et retraites*, edited by L. Arrondel. Paris: Economica.
Mill, John Stuart. 1848. *Principles of Political Economy*. London: The Macmillan Company.
North, Douglas. 1981. *Structure and Change in Economic History*. New York: Norton.
North, Douglas. 2005. *Understanding the Process of Economic Change*. Princeton: Princeton University Press.
Piketty, Thomas. 2019. *Capital and Ideology*. Cambridge: Harvard University Press.
Ponthiere, Gregory. 2017a. *Economie du vieillissement*. Paris: Editions La Découverte.
Ponthiere, Gregory. 2017b. 'Pollution, décès prématuré et compensation'. *Revue Economique* 68: 97–118.
Ponthiere, Gregory. 2020a. 'A Theory of Reverse Retirement'. *Journal of Public Economic Theory* 22: 1618–1659.
Ponthiere, Gregory. 2020b. 'Pensions and Social Justice: From Standard Retirement to Reverse Retirement'. *Revue De l'OFCE* 170: 193–226.
Prouteau, Lionel. 2018. Bénévolat et bénévoles en France en 2017: états des lieux et tendances. *Rapport de recherches du LEM*.
Samuelson, Paul. 1975. The Optimum Growth Rate for Population. *International Economic Review* 16: 531–538.
Skirbekk, Vegard. 2004. 'Age and Individual Productivity: A Literature Survey'. In *Vienna Yearbook of Population Research*, edited by G. Feichtinger. Vienna: Academy of Sciences.
Supiot, Alain. 1999. *Au-delà de l'emploi. Rapport pour la Commission Européenne*. Paris: Flammarion.
Van de Velde, Cécile. 2008. *Devenir adulte. Sociologie comparée de la jeunesse en Europe*. Paris: Presses Universitaires de France.
Van Ours, Jan, and Lenny Stoeldraijer. 2010. 'Age, Wage and Productivity'. IZA Discussion Paper 4765.
Van Parijs, Philippe, and Yannick Vanderborght. 2018. *Basic Income, A Radical Proposal for a Just Society and a Sane Economy*. Cambridge: Harvard University Press.
Viard, Jean. 2019. *Un nouvel âge jeune? Devenir adulte dans une société mobile*. Paris: Editions de l'aube.
Zhang, Jie, Jungen Zhang, and Ronald Lee. 2001. 'Mortality Decline and long-Run Economic Growth'. *Journal of Public Economics* 80: 485–507.

CHAPTER 5

Conclusion: The Welfare State at a Crossroad

Abstract It is concluded that a social insurance against a short life is socially desirable and technically feasible in advanced societies. But even if the current demographic and technical conditions constitute a unique opportunity in History, there may be strong political oppositions to a partial reversal of pension systems, especially among senior workers. Modern Welfare States are at a crossroad: either we keep on reforming the Welfare State by making it 'smaller', but also less protective, or, alternatively, we extend the domain of social insurance, in such a way as to protect citizens against the risk of a short life, the most tragic of all risks. This essay makes a policy proposal of extending the domain of social protection to the risk of a short life. As such, this essay is only a very first step toward more public debates about the scope of social protection in advanced societies.

Keywords Welfare states · Policy reforms · Social protection · Pension systems · Reverse retirement

A social insurance against the risk of a short life is possible. True, the harm due to a premature death exhibits some particularities, which impose constraints on the design of this insurance device. The victim of a premature death is not alive any longer once the harm has taken place. Hence,

G. Ponthiere, *Allocating Pensions to Younger People*, https://doi.org/10.1007/978-3-031-24748-4_5

the insurance against a short life cannot take the same form as existing social insurances, such as the unemployment insurance or the health insurance, which give compensatory allowances to victims after the occurrence of the harm. However, these obstacles can be overcome, provided one leaves one's imagination work.

This essay defended that the construction of a reverse retirement system could constitute a first step towards the realization of a social insurance against the risk of a short life. This insurance device would allow all young adults to benefit from an initial retirement period, before starting their career, a period that could be used to study, travel, flourish and, above everything, to live, to live as if the life could stop at any moment. By giving to each young adult a pension allowance financed by the work of the seniors, the welfare state would contribute to reduce the harm suffered by the few unlucky persons who die prematurely, and, hence, would provide foundations for a real insurance against a short life.[1]

The social insurance against a short life is not only possible, it is also desirable. Its existence is dictated by considerations of social justice. Our societies currently do little things for the persons who die prematurely. Worse: the current organization of work along the life cycle and the current pension systems *reinforce* the harms due to a premature death, and, hence, exacerbate well-being inequalities due to unequal longevities. This particular point must be explained—as we did in this essay—and explained again, since obstacles are numerous: the victims of a short life are invisible, and the harm due to a short life is also invisible. We must say and say again that even if a premature death can be due to fatality, the disadvantage of persons who die prematurely is *not* a fatality. The size of this harm depends on how material resources and free time are allocated along the life cycle, which is deeply related to how the production process is organized within the society. The welfare state should be reorganized, in such a way as to improve the situation of the unlucky short-lived persons as much as possible. The reversal of retirement systems can attenuate the

[1] It should be stressed that the construction of a reverse retirement system is necessary, but not sufficient to achieve the goal of providing a social insurance against the risk of a short life. The reason is twofold. First, introducing a reverse retirement system is generally not sufficient to provide a complete insurance against a short life (i.e., full compensation), in the same way as existing social insurance devices are incomplete too. Second, insuring citizens against a short life requires also dealing with the articulation of reverse retirement with the design of the other pillars of the welfare state, such as long-term care insurance (see Leroux et al. 2021).

harm due to a premature death, and make our society closer to a more just world, a world where harms and welfare losses would not be concentrated on a few persons, but, rather, would be shared equally among all humans.

The welfare state stands at a crossroad. Two roads can be taken, but these roads are orthogonal. Either the welfare state keeps its current structure and adopts a defensive strategy when facing attacks from neoliberals, without trying to extend its perimeter of action. Or, alternatively, the welfare state pursues a more ambitious goal: the extension of its domain through the construction of a new pillar of social protection: a social insurance against the risk of a short life. This reform of social security requires nothing less than the reversal of retirement systems.

Reverse retirement is also a step towards a more humane society. This is about doing justice to the nature of Man: Man is, above all, a *homo moriturus*, a being subject to a risk of death. Neither an automat, nor a machine, but a vulnerable being. A just society should not do 'as if' all its members were invulnerable. A humane economy is an economy where the scarcity of lifetime is taken seriously into account, and where institutions are organized in such a way as to take care of all lives, despite their unequal lengths.

Lucretius compared life with a meal, while Seneca used to regard life as a see cruise. Let us conclude this essay by adopting another metaphor: each life is like a pictorial composition. Some lives are short, and last only a few decades, whereas other lives are much longer, and exceed a century. In a similar way, some paintings have a small format, while others occupy plain walls. The medium—the size of the canvas—imposes its own constraints to the painter. But whatever the constraints are, each painting should be a composition in itself. Reverse retirement, by offering to each young adult an initial period of retirement free from any work necessity, would help the young seeing their life as a blank canvas, open to all forms and colours. Transforming each person into the painter of her life, into the visual artist of her existence. Making each life—even the shortest—a full-fledged composition, a unique, singular and splendid piece of art.

Reference

Leroux, Marie-Louise, Pierre Pestieau, and Gregory Ponthiere. 2021. 'Fair Long Term Care Insurance'. *Social Choice and Welfare* 57: 503–533.

Appendix

On Alternative Insurance Devices Against a Short Life

One could argue against reverse retirement that there exist other—potentially more efficient—insurance strategies reducing the volatility of lifetime well-being in the context of risky lifetime. In this section, I will review some other—existing or potential—insurance devices against the risk of a short life, and I will argue that these other devices are dominated by reverse retirement, either in terms of an insufficient ratio of insured persons over the total population at risk, or in terms of an insufficient compensation in case of a premature death.

Standard insurance devices against the risk of a short life include private life insurance contracts. Life insurance contracts require the payment, by the insured person, of insurance premium in exchange of the payment to a designated beneficiary (e.g., the spouse, children or relatives) of a benefit in case of the death of the insured person. These contracts contribute to reduce, for the insured person, well-being losses in case of a premature death, and, as such, correspond to what one expects from an insurance against a short life. In the light of this, a natural question is: if the welfare state wants to insure individuals against a short life, why not relying on standard life insurance contracts, rather than on reverse retirement?

In order to answer this question, it is necessary to underline a major characteristic of life insurance contracts: these contracts allow to reducing

G. Ponthiere, *Allocating Pensions to Younger People*,
https://doi.org/10.1007/978-3-031-24748-4

well-being losses in case of premature death if and only if the insured person derives well-being from the fact that the designated beneficiary will, in case of his death, obtain some insurance benefit. This can arise when the insured person is altruistic towards the designated beneficiary or when the insured person exhibits some 'joy of giving' with respect to the beneficiary.[1] These conditions are generally satisfied by individuals purchasing life insurance contracts.[2] But not all individuals exhibit altruism or joy of giving towards other persons. Our societies include persons who are isolated from other persons, i.e., persons who do not have family or friends. From the point of view of socially excluded persons, life insurance contracts are useless. Moreover, subsidizing life insurance contracts would not encourage isolated persons to purchase these contracts. As a consequence, standard life insurance contracts cannot lead to a full coverage of the population at risk of dying prematurely.[3]

The problem faced by standard life insurance contracts lies in the fact that these provide only *indirect* compensation for the insured persons in case of premature death. This indirect compensation takes the form of a monetary transfer towards some designated beneficiary, but not of a transfer towards the insured person. The insurance device works through providing some money transfer to another person whose well-being or material situation matters for the insured person, through altruism or joy of giving concerns. But in the absence of such a designated beneficiary, the life insurance contract cannot insure the person against the risk of premature death. As a consequence, relying on free (private) life insurance markets is unlikely to bring insurance against a short life for all citizens at risk of having a short life.

[1] Pure altruism arises when a person's utility function depends on the utility or well-being of another person. Impure or incomplete altruism takes place when a person's utility function depends on some components of another person's utility. On the contrary, in the case of joy of giving, the person derives some well-being from the mere act of giving, independently from how the beneficiary of the transfer will appreciate the gift. On the distinction between these concepts, the seminal reference is Kolm and Ythier (2006).

[2] The reason is that, in the absence of altruism or joy of giving, these persons would simply not purchase these life insurance contracts.

[3] Moreover, even if one considers persons who are not isolated from others, it should be stressed that the degree of altruism or joy of giving is generally too low to allow for a significant compensation of the deceased.

The same criticism can be formulated against another way of insuring individuals against a short life: the subsidization of bequests left by prematurely dead persons. The underlying idea behind this policy would be to reduce well-being losses due to a premature death by taxing less—or even subsidizing—the bequests transmitted by prematurely dead persons to the surviving family members or friends.[4] This policy amounts to have age-differentiated tax on inheritance, with a tax rate that increases with the age of the deceased. The rationale would go as follows: persons who die prematurely suffer from a welfare loss that can be partly compensated by allowing them to transmit *more* wealth to their family and friends.

Here again, this insurance strategy is an *indirect* compensation of the short-lived: this goes through transferring money to persons surviving after the death of the person. As a consequence, the same kind of criticism as above applies in this case: age-differentiated inheritance taxation can only be used as an insurance against a short life if and only if the persons who die prematurely exhibit altruism or joy of giving with respect to some other persons. Otherwise, in the case of socially isolated persons, this insurance strategy will fail.

In sum, indirect insurance strategies that consist of transferring money to surviving persons (for whom the deceased person cares)—either though life insurance contracts or age-differentiated inheritance taxation—do not work in the case of socially isolated persons, because the well-being of these persons does not depend on the situation of others. Indirect insurance strategies exclude de facto socially isolated persons, which leads to an insufficient coverage of the population at risk of dying prematurely.

Reverse retirement does not have this problem: this policy improves the situation of *all* short-lived persons, including the socially isolated persons, and the persons who exhibit no altruism and no joy of giving. The reason is that reverse retirement improves the situation of the prematurely dead persons *directly*, without having to rely on transfers to other persons. Allowing all young adults to enjoy the pleasures of retirement

[4] This idea was developed by Fleurbaey et al. (2022), who compare the optimal taxation of inheritance under utilitarianism and ex post egalitarianism, and show that the latter may, under some conditions, involve subsidizing the bequests left by prematurely dead persons, as a way to allow them to give more to their descendants. Note that this indirect compensation strategy works only if the degree of altruism or joy of giving of the deceased is sufficiently high, but not otherwise.

will improve the situation of all of them, including the ones who will turn out to die prematurely in the future, whether or not these persons exhibit altruism or joy of giving. Reverse retirement can thus cover the entire population at risk of dying prematurely.

On Junior Work Ban

When considering the design of a social insurance against a short life, a key issue concerns the treatment of youth labour. Reverse retirement, as presented in Chapter 4, involves a prohibition of work for young adults, in the same way as standard retirement involves a ban for the work of senior persons. But one may argue that prohibiting the work of junior persons is problematic for the goal of insuring individuals against the risk of a short life. The reason is that young persons who like consumption a lot may prefer to be able to work at the young age rather than not working, in order to be able to consume more at the young age. Reverse retirement would prevent these young persons from working, and would thus make these persons worse-off in case of a premature death.[5]

In order to examine that criticism of the junior work ban, let us compare the consequences, on realized well-being levels across the lifetime, of two variants of reverse retirement: on the one hand, reverse retirement *without* junior work ban (young persons can choose to opt out of the early retirement period), and, on the other hand, reverse retirement *with* junior work ban (young persons cannot opt out of the early retirement period). For the sake of presentation, we consider a reduced-form economy composed of persons who differ in preferences in the (consumption, leisure) space: some persons like leisure time a lot, whereas other individuals like consumption a lot. The former persons will generally work little, whereas the latter will supply more labour. Let us also suppose that the population includes persons with different attitudes towards time. Some persons are biased towards the present, and care mainly about the current period in which they live. On the contrary, other persons suffer from a bias towards the future, and assign high weight to what will happen when they will be old.[6]

[5] I thank Philippe Van Parijs for this criticism.

[6] Following Parfit (1984)'s surgery case, we have reasons to believe that the bias towards the future is much more widespread than the bias towards the present.

Table A1 shows the utility payoffs of the four types of persons, in the cases of a short life or of a long life, under the two variants of reverse retirement. The utility payoffs are represented by alphabetical letters. Several observations are in order. First, given that all letters correspond to strictly positive utility levels, long-lived persons are, *ceteris paribus*, better-off than short-lived persons. This welfare inequality is plausible in advanced economies with large consumption and leisure possibilities.[7] Second, the junior work ban has the consequence of improving the situation of the short-lived persons who like leisure, whatever these persons have a bias towards the present or a bias towards the future. Indeed, the junior work ban reduces the quantity of labour at young age, and thus increases leisure time there. For short-lived persons who like leisure a lot, this rise in the leisure time at young age is welfare-improving. Third, the junior work ban has a negative effect on persons who like consumption a lot and are biased towards the present, and turn out to die prematurely. Indeed, these young persons would like to consume a lot now, and, thus, preventing them from working and consuming now reduces their lifetime welfare. But the junior work ban has a positive effect on young persons who like consumption, are biased towards the future and turn out to die prematurely. The reason is that these persons would, in the absence of the junior work ban, have worked a lot and saved much to the old age. Unfortunately, in case of premature death, these persons would not enjoy the old age, making all their efforts useless.

When considering all these inequalities, it appears that the introduction of a junior work ban has a mixed effect on the realized welfare of the short-lived, an effect whose sign varies with the preferences of the persons (leisure-lover or consumption-lover). But despite this mixed effect, it is nonetheless possible to deduce something about the effect of the junior work ban on the realized well-being of the *worst-off* person. To see this, it is crucial to notice that, whether one considers leisure-lovers or consumption-lovers, it is always the case that, among the short-lived, persons who are biased towards the future are worse-off than persons who are biased towards the present. The reason is that persons who are biased towards the future make efforts and sacrifices for the old age, which is catastrophic in case of a premature death.

[7] On this assumption, see Fleurbaey et al. (2014).

Table A1 A comparison of reverse retirement with/without junior work ban

		Reverse retirement without junior work ban		*Reverse retirement with junior work ban*	
		Short life	*Long life*	*Short life*	*Long life*
Leisure-lover	Bias towards present	a	$a + b$	$c > a$	$c + d$
Leisure-lover	Bias towards future	$e < a$	$e + f$	$e < g < c$	$g + h$
Consumption-lover	Bias towards present	i	$i + j$	$k < i$	$k + l$
Consumption-lover	Bias towards future	$m < i$	$m + n$	$m < o < k$	$o + p$

Once it is acknowledged that the short-lived persons who were biased towards the future are worse-off than the persons (with similar preferences) biased towards the present, it appears that the worst-off persons in our population consist of short-lived leisure-lovers and consumption-lovers who are biased towards the future. *Interestingly, in the case of persons biased towards the future, the introduction of a junior work ban is always welfare-improving*. Indeed, the ban prevents leisure-lovers from working more at the young age to secure more leisure time at older ages, and this ban prevents also consumption-lovers from working more at the young age to secure higher consumption in the future. Thus, whatever the persons biased towards the future are leisure-lovers or consumption-lovers, the ban on junior labour makes these persons better-off in case of a premature death, in comparison to the absence of the junior work ban. As a consequence, given that these persons are the most disadvantaged in our economy, it follows from egalitarian concerns that a device aimed at reducing welfare losses for the short-lived must include a ban on youth work.

This discussion illustrates that reverse retirement systems allowing or prohibiting junior work bans have different consequences on the realized lifetime welfare of short-lived persons. In the presence of a bias towards the future, it is crucial to impose a junior work ban, in such a way as to avoid situations where young individuals sacrifice present times for the sake of securing more leisure or consumption in the future, something they will never enjoy in case of a premature death.

This result may seem surprising. Indeed, imposing a ban or a prohibition amounts to *reduce* the number of options available in the menu when the person must choose how to plan her life, how to allocate leisure time and consumption along the life cycle. One may thus be tempted to believe that reducing the menu will always reduce realized welfare, and, as such, should not be carried out. But our analysis shows the opposite: from the perspective of maximizing the realized welfare of the most disadvantaged persons (the short-lived persons who suffered from a bias towards the future), it is optimal to reduce the number of available options when planning one's life, in order to avoid having individuals making mistakes. Among all possible mistakes, the most serious ones concern persons biased towards the future, who want to transfer lots of goods to the old age, but cannot reach it. This explains why it is optimal, from the perspective of the well-being of the worst-off, to impose a junior work ban.

From a liberal perspective, imposing a junior work ban may seem paternalistic, and, thus, unjustified, on the grounds that it prevents some young individuals from doing what they plan to do in their own life. However, our analysis suggests that there is, from an egalitarian perspective, a strong support for imposing a junior work ban, especially in a context where individuals exhibit a bias towards the future. The bias towards the future pushes young persons who turn out to be short-lived to make serious mistakes, which deprive them significantly of well-being. The construction of a social insurance against a short life aims precisely at reducing these well-being losses, and this can be best achieved by imposing a junior work ban. As a consequence, if one wants to construct a social insurance against the risk of premature death, a reverse retirement system including a junior work ban dominates a reverse retirement system without junior work ban.

References

Fleurbaey, Marc, Marie-Louise Leroux, Pierre Pestieau, Gregory Ponthiere, and Stephane Zuber. 2022. 'Premature Deaths, Accidental Bequests and Fairness'. *Scandinavian Journal of Economics* 124: 709–743.

Fleurbaey, Marc, Marie-Louise Leroux, and Gregory Ponthiere. 2014. 'Compensating the Dead'. *Journal of Mathematical Economics* 51: 28–41.

Kolm, Serge-Christophe, and Jean-Mercier Ythier. 2006. *Handbook of the Economics of Giving, Altruism and Reciprocity*. Amsterdam: North-Holland.

Parfit, Derek. 1984. *Reasons and Persons*. Oxford: Oxford University Press.

Bibliography

Ackerman, Bruce, and Anne Alstott. 1999. *The Stakeholder Society*. New Haven: Yale University Press.

Ariès, Philippe. 1974. *Western Attitudes Toward Death*. Baltimore: Johns Hopkins University Press.

Arrow, Kenneth. 1965. *Aspects of the Theory of Risk-Bearing*. Helsinki: Yrjo Johnsson Lectures.

Atkinson, Anthony. 2015. *Inequality: What Can Be Done?* Cambridge, MA: Harvard University Press.

Aubert, Patrick, and Bruno Crépon. 2003. 'La productivité des salariés âgés: Une tentative d'estimation'. *Economie et Prévisions* 368: 95–119.

Bachelard, Gaston. 1931. *L'intuition de l'instant*. Paris: Vrin, English version *The Intuition of the Instant*, translated by Eileen Rizo-Praton, 2000.

Bachelard, Gaston. 1938. *La formation de l'esprit scientifique*. Paris: Vrin.

Bachelard, Gaston. 1950. *La dialectique de la durée*. Paris: Presses Universitaires de France, English version *The Dialectics of Duration*, translated by Mary McAllester Jones, 2013.

Balia, Silvia, and Andrew Jones. 2008. 'Mortality, Lifestyles and Socioeconomic Status'. *Journal of Health Economics* 27: 1–26.

Barr, Nicholas, and Peter Diamond. 2003. 'The Economics of Pensions'. *Oxford Review of Economic Policy* 22: 15–39.

Barr, Nicholas, and Peter Diamond. 2008. *Reforming Pensions*. Oxford: Oxford University Press.

Bentham, Jeremy. 1789. *An Introdution to the Principles of Morals and Legislation*. Oxford: Clarendon Press.

G. Ponthiere, *Allocating Pensions to Younger People*,
https://doi.org/10.1007/978-3-031-24748-4

Berg, Joyce, John Dickhaut, and Kevin McCabe. 1995. 'Trust, Reciprocity, and Social History'. *Games and Economic Behaviour* 10: 122–142.

Blanchet, Didier. 2007. 'Perspectives démographiques et marché du travail: quelle relation?' In *Les retraites: libres opinions d'experts européens*, edited by F. Legros. Paris: Economica.

Bommier, Antoine, Thierry Magnac, Benoît Rapoport, and Muriel Roger. 2006. 'Droits à la retraite et mortalité différentielle'. *Economie et Prévisions* 168: 1–16.

Bozio, Antoine, and Thomas Piketty. 2008. *Pour un nouveau système de retraites*. Paris: Editions rue d'Ulm.

Bradley, Ben. 2009. *Well-Being and Death*. Oxford: Oxford University Press.

Broome, John. 1999. *Ethics Out of Economics*. Cambridge: Cambridge University Press.

Broome, John. 2004. *Weighing Lives*. Oxford: Oxford University Press.

Christensen, Kaare, Thomas Johnson, and James Vaupel. 2006. 'The Quest for Genetic Determinants of Human Longevity: Challenges and Insights'. *Nature Genetics* 7: 436–448.

Coronado, Julia Lynn, Don Fullerton, and Thomas Glass. 2011. 'The Progressivity of Social Security'. *The B.E. Journal of Economic Analysis and Policy* 11: 1–45.

Cremer, Helmuth, and Pierre Pestieau. 2011. 'Myopia, Redistribution and Pensions'. *European Economic Review* 55: 165–175.

D'Albis, Hippolyte, Angela Greulich, and Gregory Ponthiere. 2015. *Avoir un enfant plus tard. Enjeux sociodémographiques du report des naissances*. Paris: Editions rue d'Ulm.

Epicurus, *Letter to Menoeceus*. English version translated by Cyril Bailey, 1926.

Finkelstein, Amy, and Katherine McGarry. 2006. 'Multiple Dimensions of Private Information: Evidence from the Long-Term Care Insurance Market'. *American Economic Review* 96: 938–958.

Fleurbaey, Marc. 2009. *Fairness, Responsibility and Welfare*. Oxford: Oxford University Press.

Fleurbaey, Marc, Marie-Louise Leroux, Pierre Pestieau, and Gregory Ponthiere. 2016. 'Fair Retirement Under Risky Lifetime'. *International Economic Review* 57: 177–210.

Fleurbaey, Marc, Marie-Louise Leroux, Pierre Pestieau, Gregory Ponthiere, and Stephane Zuber. 2022. 'Premature Deaths, Accidental Bequests and Fairness'. *Scandinavian Journal of Economics* 124: 709–743.

Fleurbaey, Marc, Marie-Louise Leroux, and Gregory Ponthiere. 2014. 'Compensating the Dead'. *Journal of Mathematical Economics* 51: 28–41.

Fleurbaey, Marc, and Gregory Ponthiere. 2022a. 'The Value of a Life-year and the Intuition of Universality'. *Journal of Ethics and Social Philosophy* 22: 355–381.

Fleurbaey, Marc, and Gregory Ponthiere. 2022b. 'Measuring Well-being and Lives Worth Living'. *Economic Theory*, forthcoming.

Galor, Oded. 2011. *Unified Growth Theory*. Princeton: Princeton University Press.

Genet, Michel, and Philippe Van Parijs. 1992. 'Eurogrant'. *Basic Income Research Group Bulletin* 15: 4–7.

Jankelevitch, Vladimir. 1977. *La mort*. Paris: Flammarion.

Jevons, William Stanley. 1874. *The Theory of Political Economy*. London: Pellican Books.

Kahneman, Daniel. 2011. *Thinking, Fast and Slow*. London: Allen Lane.

Kamm, Frances. 1993. *Morality, Mortality*, vol. 1. Oxford: Oxford University Press.

Kolm, Serge-Christophe, and Jean-Mercier Ythier. 2006. *Handbook of the Economics of Giving, Altruism and Reciprocity*. Amsterdam: North-Holland.

Laroque, Pierre. 1948. 'De l'assurance sociale à la sécurité sociale: l'expérience sociale'. *Revue Internationale du Travail* LVII : 621–649

Lavigne, Anne. 2013. *Economie des retraites*. Paris: Editions La Découverte.

Leroux, Marie-Louise, Pierre Pestieau, and Gregory Ponthiere. 2021. 'Fair Long Term Care Insurance'. *Social Choice and Welfare* 57: 503–533.

Lee, Ronald. 2003. 'The Demographic Transition: Three Centuries of Fundamental Change'. *Journal of Economic Perspectives*, 17: 167–190.

Lippert-Rasmussen, Kasper. 2018. 'Discriminations'. *Oxford Handbook of Distributive Justice*. Oxford: Oxford University Press.

Lucretius. 2015. *On the Nature of Things*. Translated by William Ellery Leonard. London: J. M. Dent & Sons.

MacMahan, Jeff. 2002. *The Ethics of Killing: Problems at the Margin of Life*. Oxford: Oxford University Press.

Marx, Karl. 1875. *Critique of the Gotha Program*. New York: International Publishers.

Masson, André. 2003. 'Redistribution et équité intergénérationnelle'. In *Epargne, assurance-vie et retraites*, edited by L. Arrondel. Paris: Economica.

Meyer, Patrick, and Gregory Ponthiere. 2020. 'Human Lifetime Entropy in a Historical Perspective (1750–2014)'. *Cliometrica* 14: 129–167.

Mill, John Stuart. 1848. *Principles of Political Economy*. London: The Macmillan Company.

Miller, David. 1976. *Social Justice*. Oxford: Oxford University Press.

Mirrlees, James. 1982. 'The Economic Uses of Utilitarianism'. In *Utilitarianism and Beyond*, edited by A.K. Sen and B. Williams. Cambridge: Cambridge University Press.

Moore, G.E. 1912. *Principia Ethica*. Cambridge: Cambridge University Press.

Nagel, Thomas. 1979. *Mortal Questions*. Cambridge: Cambridge University Press.

North, Douglas. 1981. *Structure and Change in Economic History*. New York: Norton.

North, Douglas. 2005. *Understanding the Process of Economic Change*. Princeton: Princeton University Press.

Parfit, Derek. 1984. *Reasons and Persons*. Oxford: Oxford University Press.

Pasolini, Pier-Paolo. 1962. *Il Sogno di Una Cosa*. French version. Le rêve d'une chose: Gallimard, 1962.

Pestieau, Pierre, and Gregory Ponthiere. 2012. 'Long Term Care Insurance Puzzle'. In *Financing Long-Term Care in Europe: Institutions, Markets and Models*, edited by J. Costa-Font and C. Courbage. Basingstoke: Palgrave Macmillan.

Pigou, Arthur Cecil. 1920. *The Economics of Welfare*. London: Macmillan.

Piketty, Thomas. 2019. *Capital and Ideology*. Cambridge: Harvard University Press.

Ponthiere, Gregory. 2017a. *Economie du vieillissement*. Paris: Editions La Découverte.

Ponthiere, Gregory. 2017b. 'Pollution, décès prématuré et compensation'. *Revue Economique* 68: 97–118.

Ponthiere, Gregory. 2020a. 'A Theory of Reverse Retirement'. *Journal of Public Economic Theory* 22: 1618–1659.

Ponthiere, Gregory. 2020b. 'Pensions and Social Justice: From Standard Retirement to Reverse Retirement'. *Revue de l'OFCE* 170: 193–226.

Prouteau, Lionel, 2018. Bénévolat et bénévoles en France en 2017: états des lieux et tendances. Rapport de recherches du LEM.

Rawls, John. 1971. *A Theory of Justice*. Cambridge: Harvard University Press.

Rifkin, Jeremy. 1995. *The End of Work*. New York: Putnam Publishing Group.

Samuelson, Paul. 1975. 'The Optimum Growth Rate for Population'. *International Economic Review* 16: 531–538.

Sen, Amartya. 1977. 'Rational Fools: A Critique of the Behavioural Foundations of Economic Theory'. *Philosophy and Public Affairs* 6: 317–344.

Sen, Amartya. 1980. 'Equality of What?' *Tanner Lectures on Human Values*. Utah: University of Utah Press.

Sen, Amartya. 1998. 'Mortality as an Indicator of Economic Success and Failure'. *Economic Journal* 100: 1–21.

Seneca. 2014. *On the Shortness of Life*. Translated by Gareth D. Williams.

Skirbekk, Vegard. 2004. 'Age and Individual Productivity: A Literature Survey'. In *Vienna Yearbook of Population Research*, edited by G. Feichtinger. Vienna: Academy of Sciences.

Sterdyniak, Henri. 2009. 'Retraites: à la recherche de solutions miracles'. *Revue de l'OFCE* 109: 109–140.

Supiot, Alain. 1999. *Au-delà de l'emploi. Rapport pour la Commission Européenne*. Paris: Flammarion.

Van de Velde, Cécile. 2008. *Devenir adulte. Sociologie comparée de la jeunesse en Europe*. Paris: Presses Universitaires de France.
Van Ours, Jan, and Lenny Stoeldraijer. 2010. 'Age, Wage and Productivity'. IZA Discussion Paper 4765.
Van Parijs Philippe, and Yannick Vanderborght. 2018. *Basic Income, a Radical Proposal for a Just Society and a Sane Economy*. Cambridge: Harvard University Press.
Viard, Jean. 2019. *Un nouvel âge jeune? Devenir adulte dans une société mobile*. Paris: Editions de l'aube.
Warren, James. 2004. *Facing Death: Epicurus and His Critics*. Oxford: Oxford University Press.
Wittgenstein, Ludwig. 1922. *Tractatus Logico-Philosophicus*. New York: Kegan Paul.
Zhang, Jie, Jungen Zhang, and Ronald Lee. 2001. 'Mortality Decline and long-Run Economic Growth'. *Journal of Public Economics* 80: 485–507.
Zweifel, Peter, and Roland Eisen. 2012. *Insurance Economics*. Heidelberg: Springer.

Index

G. Ponthiere, *Allocating Pensions to Younger People*,
https://doi.org/10.1007/978-3-031-24748-4

W

Y

www.ingramcontent.com/pod-product-compliance
Ingram Content Group UK Ltd.
Pitfield, Milton Keynes, MK11 3LW, UK
UKHW021031041026
15470UKWH00014B/1391

* 9 7 8 3 0 3 1 2 4 7 4 7 7 *